MW01600301

FINAL DOOM

The Frederick Hollman Story

FINAL DOOM

The Frederick Hollman Story

By

KEVIN COLLIER

Black Oak
M E D I A

Final Doom: The Frederick Hollman Story

Copyright © 2012 by Kevin Scott Collier
Cover illustration: Frederick Hollman, © 1897 Chicago Tribune
Photo of Hollman on the Gallows was taken by Olaf Rasmus in 1897 and first published in *Ford County Centennial Edition* (1959)
Interior Design by Michael Kleen

First Edition published by Black Oak Media, Inc. in 2012

All rights reserved. No part of this book may be reproduced or transmitted in any form or by any means including photocopying, recording, or by any information storage and retrieval system, without written permission from the copyright owner, except for the inclusion of brief quotations in an article or review.

First Printing Summer 2012

ISBN-13: 978-1-61876-008-1

Published by Black Oak Media

1. History—Midwest. 2. Frederick Hollman. 3. True Crime. 4. American Serial Killers.

To order copies of this book contact:

Black Oak Media, Inc.
Rockford, Illinois
www.blackoakmedia.org
orders@blackoakmedia.org

Printed in the United States of America.

Special Thanks*:*

The author wishes to thank all of the fine and kind historians from Ford County, Illinois and surrounding counties, contacts in Wisconsin and here at home in Grand Haven, Michigan, including:

Marcie Shaffer and Karen Moen of the Bloomington Public Library, Illinois

The Princeton Historical Society, Wisconsin

Gail Hahn Hutchcraft, (Ladybug), Ford County Historian

Rosemary Kurtz, Paxton Carnegie Library Historian

Barbara King of the Ford County Sheriff's Office, Illinois

Mary Runyon-Hanshew of Chatsworth Illinois Memories

Marilyn Gahm Ames, retired history teacher, Melvin-Sibley Jr-Sr High School

Judy Schall, V.P, Melvin Public Library Board, Illinois

The Paxton Public Library, Illinois

The Guthrie Memorial Library, Pennsylvania

The Gilman Historical Society, Illinois

Lee County Historical Society, Illinois

The Urbana Free Library, Illinois

The Gibson City Courier newspaper, Illinois

The Paxton Record newspaper, Illinois

The Pantagraph daily newspaper, Bloomington, Illinois

The Melvin Transcript newspaper, Illinois

The Sibley Journal newspaper, Illinois

Chatsworth Plain Dealer newspaper, Illinois

The Chicago Tribune newspaper, Illinois

The New York Times, New York

The Milwaukee Journal, Wisconsin

The Milwaukee Sentinel, Wisconsin

Eau Claire Leader newspaper, Wisconsin

The Telegraph-Courier newspaper, Wisconsin

The Racine Journal newspaper, Wisconsin

The Kenosha Evening News newspaper, Wisconsin

The Grand Haven Tribune, Michigan

Dodge County Information Technology, Juneau, Wisconsin

The Gilman Historical Society, Illinois

Bob Beaton of Sand Hill City website, Michigan

Wallace K. Ewing, Grand Haven Historian and author

Michael J. Rohloff of Lake Forest Cemetery, Grand Haven, Michigan

Three descendants of Frederick William Hollman

Donald Hilgendorf, descendant of August and Bertha Hilgendorf

Brent Schmid, descendant of Albert and Carrie Lenz

Royce Baier, President of the Paxton Foundation

www.melvinillinois.org

www.familysearch.org

Ford County Jailhouse, 1897

Contents

INTRODUCTION
THE OTHER H. H. HOLMES

Frederick Hollman, the Forgotten Serial Killer

The story of Frederich Wilhelm Hoellmann, or Frederick William Hollman, begins when his first wife Amelia and he arrived in America and settled in Grand Haven, Michigan. You might imagine his story ended with his death in Paxton, Illinois, at the gallows, but it did not. The story, in fact, continues to this day.

Hollman was executed in Ford County, Illinois on May 14, 1897. While he was convicted of only one murder, at least six are attributed to him during a 13 month period between 1895 and 1896. Some newspapers reported the number of Hollman's victims could have been as many as 17.

Frederick William Hollman became one of our nation's first serial killers on the heels of the man criminologists define as the first—H. H. Holmes. Hollman was executed for his crimes one year after Holmes was hanged. So, how is it that Frederick Hollman has been overlooked by historians?

Descendants of Frederick Hollman (many of whom were interviewed for this book) were unknowingly subjects of a 114-year compassionate deception. Hollman's estranged wife, to protect their young children, informed them that their father had perished in a train accident in Chicago, around 1900. This fable would endure until Hollman's descendants were contacted during research for this book in 2010. Only then would they discover the truth—that their ancestor was a serial killer.

Descendants of victims still remain in the dark concerning the loss of their distant ancestors. One family, the Hilgendorfs, have endured the century-old shame of a relative wrongly convicted of murder, a crime to which Hollman had privately confessed.

The man whom the press called "another Holmes," who went to his grave never making a public confession, who authored an egotistical poem titled "Legendary," and whose

Kevin Collier

greatest aim was to live on in infamy, instead slipped away into silent obscurity.

"To America I journeyed, in honest to toll, and now they gonna hang me, and raise a great turmoil," Hollman wrote in his self-serving poem. "On 14 day of May, when flowers are in bloom, between sunrise and sunset, I must meet my fatal doom."

And now...Hollman's final doom can be revealed for the first time.

—Kevin Collier

PART 1

Hollman Comes to America

Frederich Wilhelm Hoellman, born in 1859 to Charles and Augusta Hoellman, was raised in the small village of Leonars in a northern part of Brandenburg, Germany near the river Rhine.

He married Amelia Cards around 1880. The couple departed Germany in early 1883 arriving in the United States at Ellis Island, New York. From there they traveled to Michigan and settled in the city of Grand Haven where Friedrich had two cousins who had immigrated to America earlier.

He was 24-years-old upon his arrival in the city.

A German settlement in the port city of Grand Haven was a popular starting point for many immigrants of that origin at the time. The community of Berlin, Michigan, some 15 miles to the east, had the largest population of German immigrants in Ottawa County during this period.

"Some of the citizens of Grand Haven township are a peculiar class of people," the Grand Haven Tribune said in an article published in 1894. "There are three distinct communities in the township - Irishville, Germantown and Polacktown."

Frederich's cousin Charles Hoellman and his wife Augusta had arrived in Grand Haven a year earlier in July 1882. Charles Hoellman, or Charlie Hallman as he was known, was born in 1852 in Brandenburg, Germany. He married in there 1876.

Charlie and his wife Augusta owned a home on Jackson Street, where in December 1883 their first child was born, William. Charlie was a farm hand by trade but had a taken a job with the Grand Trunk Railway working himself up to the position of car inspector.

Another cousin, Carl Hoellman, brother to Charlie, who also went by the last name of Hallman, came to Grand Haven in 1880 with his wife Augusta. A son named August, had been born the previous year in Germany.

Carl and Augusta had two children born in Grand Haven; Carl in 1884 and Manny in 1886. Carl Hallman was approximately the same age as Frederich.

Upon their arrival in the city, Frederich and Amelia Hoellman briefly stayed with Charlie Hallman until finding a residence of their own.

Frederich Wilhelm Hoellman would eventually change his name to Frederick William Hollman. However, those in the city would know him as "William." Many of documents on record list his name as "Wm. Holman" during his years in Grand Haven.

Frederick and Amelia became members of St. Paul's German Evangelical Lutheran Church of Grand Haven. The church was newly established and had opened the the same year of their arrival. The Reverend Christopher Zimmerman led the congregation, which was established by a splinter group of defectors from St. John's German Lutheran church in the city.

Members also included Frederick Hollman's two cousins and their families.

Hollman and his wife Amelia spoke fluid German and knew little English. But Frederick was not an ignorant man, according to those who knew him well. He was relatively well educated and enjoyed reading books and writing poetry.

He was a very opinionated religious man who often used the teachings of his faith to pass dark judgment on others. His self-righteous emotional outbursts often blinded him to his own harsh and sinful nature.

Many people were complimentary if not envious in regard to his singing. Hollman was said to have "a strong and clear voice" when it came to belting out hymns in church.

By most accounts, Hollman was a hard worker. He earned his livelihood as a farmhand harvesting crops and occasionally sold small livestock. His first job of merit in his newfound home was in the employ of Peter Wilds, a 38-year-old brick mason. Wilds was a Civil War veteran having served with the 6th Michigan Calvary.

"At the time (I hired him) he could barely speak English," Wilds once told the Grand Haven Tribune.

By accounts, Hollman worked well as a mason and learned how to plaster from Wilds. The work included residential and commercial projects throughout Grand Haven.

Farm work was seasonal and Frederick routinely hung out at the Grand Haven docks seeking additional employment. It paid off, and in a very short time Hollman was earning a reputation and partial living as a crewman for vessels working out of the city's shipping port.

Hollman worked on several schooners and cargo vessels operating on Lake Michigan, the most notable being the side wheel iron passenger ship The City of Milwaukee.

The passenger vessel's route allowed Hollman the means to visit a brother who lived in Ripon, Wisconsin. Julius Hoellman, who went by the last name of Hallman and was a few years younger, lived near the city of Ripon. Frederick would often stay with Julius at times during layovers at the Milwaukee port.

The City of Milwaukee passenger ship was new and put into service by The Goodrich Transportation Company the same year Frederick arrived in Grand Haven. Destination ports included Port Huron, Michigan, Chicago, Illinois, and Milwaukee, Wisconsin.

The work of a sailor was said to be "grueling" and it often kept Hollman away from his home. The job did not provide steady income, either, for the ship did not operate during the harshest of winter months.

Hollman also worked for a period in a freight house near the Grand Haven harbor. It seemed at times finding work was often a job by itself, so Frederick Hollman and his wife lived in poverty.

Hollman once said he "always gave satisfaction to his employers" wherever he had worked. He also claimed to be honest and had "never stole anything" in his life. From accounts of others at the time, this appeared to be true.

Frederick Hollman possessed a peculiar appearance. Newspapers described him as having ill-formed hands and a pear-shaped head. There was little projection from the back of his head, almost as if it were flat.

He was said to weigh no more than 135 pounds and was of average height. He routinely stooped in posture, which caused him to appear to be shorter.

His forehead retreated and his eyes were described as "mild," except when he was excited and they assumed a "vindictive gleam." His habitual glances from side to side were furtive and described as being "suspicious."

His ears were said to be set far back towards the rear of his head. Directly beneath his ears his jawbones articulated a defined and solid structure of the skull.

His nasal bone and upper jaw appeared protruded, whereas his chin receded. The mustache he wore was bushy and rendered a look of severity to his face. His facial profile was said to be sharp and "form an angle with the apex being his nose."

He used broken English when speaking with citizens of the city who did not share his native tongue. He often stammered in a manner that made it difficult for others to understand him.

Hollman reportedly had a peculiar walk accentuated by his stoop in posture. With his shoulders and head bent forward, he appeared to be hurried or anxious. The awkward stride "gave (him) the appearance of uncertainty," one observer said.

He often appeared to be preoccupied and paid little attention to where he was going.

Hollman's nature was said to be restless. He was described as being "very arrogant, and vain." Hollman's emotions could go from high spiritualism to violent episodes of anger. People who knew him warned "you wouldn't want to set him off" or "rile him" about anything.

Soon after settling in Grand Haven, Hollman gained a reputation for mistreating his wife Amelia. "He abused her in a terrible manner," the Grand Haven Tribune reported. The repeated abusive behavior gave him "a very black reputation" in the community, the newspaper added.

However, later in life Hollman would say that his time with Amelia were "the best days" of his life.

Hollman could be very compassionate at times. It was said sentimental poetry could bring tears to his eyes. People who were closest to him claimed he was a "deeply religious man," if he put his temper aside.

Little is known about his wife Amelia, including her age. One document places Amelia Hollman's birth year as 1846. If correct, she was 13 years older than Frederick.

It is possible the record had a numerical error and the year 1856 was intended.

Amelia Hollman was an avid church attendee and volunteer. She was a stay-at-home housewife who never was gainfully employed outside her home. However, she did perform house cleaning services for a chosen few, likely members of St. Paul's Evangelical Lutheran Church. The work provided for some additional household income.

On April 11, 1884, Frederick and Amelia Hollman had a child, a daughter, which they named Minnie. Minnie Hollman was baptized on the day of her birth. The Christening took place in St. Paul's German Evangelical Lutheran Church, performed by Reverend Christopher Zimmerman.

Hollman's cousin Charlie and his wife also brought a daughter into the world given the name Minnie, born in 1885.

Frederick Hollman missed work for some weeks during the summer of 1886 when his daughter Minnie took ill. She died on August 31, 1886 at the age of 2 years 4 months.

Typhoid, scarlet fever, and tuberculosis were the most common contributors of childhood deaths in Ottawa County during that period, and likely the cause of Minnie's death.

Minnie Hollman was initially buried in a plot in Lake Forest Cemetery owned by friend and St. Paul's German Evangelical Lutheran Church member, Frederick Roese. Roese would become the Pastor of the church two years later.

Shortly after Minnie's death, Hollman came up with enough money to purchase a "family plot" in Grand Haven's Lake Forest Cemetery. The land bordered the Roese plot situated one row below. The size of the plot accommodated three graves.

Minnie Hollman was quietly exhumed and moved to a final resting place in the Hollman plot that fall. However, the cemetery record was not updated to reflect the move. Thus, to this day, the note card of her burial location erroneously places her in the Roese plot.

The spring of 1885 brought with it new hope for the grieving parents. Amelia Hollman discovered she was pregnant with their second child. But tragedy would strike again and this time Frederick Hollman would be left alone.

On November 12, 1887, Amelia Hollman died during childbirth and the child was stillborn. Ottawa County death records listed Amelia's age at death to be 41 but no record exists as to whether the child was a boy or girl.

Two days after the tragedy, on November 12, Amelia Hollman was buried with the stillborn inside her coffin in the Hollman plot at Lake Forest Cemetery. They were buried beside Minnie Hollman, leaving one burial space in the plot unoccupied.

Hollman would recognize the stillborn as "a child," and said so. He would tell others later in his life, "I have a wife and *two* children buried in the cemetery at that place."

In as little as four years as a resident of Grand Haven, Frederick Hollman had lost his entire family. Those who knew him at the time wrote that Hollman's years with Amelia and Minnie were, for better or worse, the only time he felt truly "alive."

After his wife's passing, Hollman always expressed his love for Amelia whenever he spoke of her, even to those who knew he had abused her. It was reported that "the love he expressed for his wife seemed to be the only human sentiment he entertained."

But that was the love for his *first* wife.

In less than nine months, Frederick Hollman remarried.

The next woman in Hollman's life would reignite his abusive nature and the violence would escalate.

Her name was Augusta Pauline Rohde, born in Nikolskoer, near Berlin, Germany on November 27, 1868. She arrived in American with her sister Albertine in 1887 and settled in the Neshkoro and Princeton area of Wisconsin where Marquette and Green Lake Counties meet.

Augusta, or "Gusta" as she was known, was of seven children born to John (Johann) and Anna Karoline Rhode.

Letters seem to indicate a brother named August Rohde, who lived in St. Paul, Minnesota at the time, had provided passage money for the pair.

Their mother, born Anna Karoline Sommerfeldt in 1834, stayed in her homeland of Germany and would not join her children in Green Lake County until 1902 sometime after being widowed.

Records indicate Rohde and Sommerfeldt relations living in Marquette, Green Lake and Fond du Lac Counties when the sisters arrived. It also appears one relative, a "Sommerfeldt," had been one of 16 men who founded and established St. John's Evangelical Lutheran Church in 1864.

It is very likely Frederick Hollman met Augusta Rohde at St. John's Evangelical Lutheran Church. She was just 19 years of age, he was 29.

Frederick often stayed with his brother Julius Hallman, who lived in Ripon, during stops in Wisconsin as a crewman aboard the Crosby ship line. Julius would have been a member of the church, and Frederick would have attended services with him.

Julius, who went by the last name of Hallman, was born in Brandenburg, Germany in 1861.

After striking up a relationship, Augusta Rohde departed Wisconsin with Frederick Hollman for a new life in Michigan. The pair boarded a passenger steamer to Grand Haven where they were married on August 9, 1888.

The wedding ceremony was small, taking place at St. Paul's German Evangelical Lutheran Church. Frederick Roese, who had just become pastor, officiated. Witnesses Carl Hallman, a cousin of Fredererick, and family friend Carl W. Hass, both signed the marriage certificate.

As Frederick's wife, Augusta became a member of St. Paul's German Evangelical Lutheran Church.

By all accounts, Frederick Hollman and Augusta did not get along from the start. No sooner had Hollman exchanged vows with her he told friends that Gusta was "a woman of bad character," and that he knew her to "be as such when (they were) married."

Augusta Hollman was a housewife who occasionally did housework outside the home to assist with family income. Sometimes this involved doing laundry for others.

Townfolk never got to know Augusta well, because circumstances would have the Hollmans on the move shortly after their marriage.

Frederick Hollman's violent side remerged and those closest to the couple observed "he began taking to beating his wife." They had witnessed this before with Amelia.

Friends, acquaintances and members of St. Paul's church had enough of Hollman's abusive nature and at once an angry mob of Germans confronted him for beating Augusta. It was said their intentions were "to lynch the abusive man," the Grand Haven Tribune reported.

Frederick Hollman had worn out his welcome in the city. With the community shunning him, and the discovery that fall Augusta was pregnant, Frederick made a decision it was time to leave Grand Haven.

In early 1889 the Hollmans departed Grand Haven and moved to Fond du Lac County, Wisconsin, and briefly stayed with Frederick's brother Julius Hallman in the city of Ripon. Soon they relocated into their own residence nearby in Princeton, Green Lake County.

Milwaukee's German-American population at the time was more than 40%. The area was known as "the German Athens." Green Lake County was a large haven for German immigrants as well. Even today it is estimated that over 43% of Wisconsin's population can trace its origin back to Germany.

The move to Wisconsin meant a fresh start for Hollmans, but in a familiar place. Augusta's sister Albertine lived nearby, and other Rohde and Sommerfeldt relations. However, their marriage remained a turbulent one.

What started in Grand Haven would come to a finish in Princeton.

Hollman's "controlling demeanor" had grown more intense since departure from Grand Haven. His work away from home as a farmhand and travels from port to port as a sailor on Lake Michigan fostered suspicion. Augusta was well liked, and her perceived freedom and independent nature did not sit well with Frederick. Resentment followed.

Frederick Hollman was welcomed as a member of St. John's Evangelical Lutheran Church in Princeton but his hostile demeanor toward his wife soon had the congregation talking.

Evidence suggests this created a contentious situation concerning Frederick making him feel as if a stranger at the church, not a member.

Years later, when Frederick was in dire straits, he reached out to St. Paul's Church in Grand Haven for help, not St. John's in Princeton. This fostered some resentment toward his own faith, even though he imagined himself a man deeply devoted to scripture.

In Grand Haven Frederick Hollman had been one of the earliest members of St. Paul's German Evangelical Lutheran Church the year it formed. Even though he departed under unpleasant circumstances, he often indicated St. Paul's was "his" church.

The pastor at St. John's Evangelical Church in Princeton was Adolph G. Hoyer. Born in May 1856, Adolph was the son of the previous pastor, John August Hoyer, who served the congregation for 20 years.

Frederick was not a part of that history.

Adolph Hoyer resided in Princeton with his wife Carla and their two children, Oswald and Clara. His father and he were held in high regard in the city and surrounding area.

It is likely Frederick's ego would not allow him to like the man, indicated by the fact that Hoyer was never once mentioned in printed Hollman recollections.

On June 3, 1889, Frederick and Augusta Hollman brought their first child into the world, a daughter whom Frederick named Minnie after his first daughter by wife Amelia.

It was said Frederick never got over the death of his first child. Naming his second daughter after the one he buried back in Grand Haven supports that notion.

Starting a second family did not heal the loss or change his heart, and his hatred of Augusta began growing out of control.

In his mind, seeing Augusta have a social life in "her" church and with "her" friends enraged him. He did not approve of her leaving the house. Prone to jealousy, Hollman unjustly accused his wife of engaging in "affairs" when he was away on work.

It came to a head in 1890 when Frederick Hollman was arrested by police for severely beating his wife.

News of the assault made the local papers, one reporting that Hollman was jailed for "nearly beating her to death." It was revealed also that Frederick had been "threatening to hang her."

The proverbial black cat was out of the bag and the incident became a subject of hearsay and gossip.

In Augusta Hollman's statement to authorities, she explained Frederick not only told her he intended to hang her but compelled her to "watch him practice" the technique "by hanging a dog."

Authorities found no physical evidence Hollman had placed a rope or cord around his wife's neck. He had beaten her with his fists causing severe injuries, but the "hanging display" was determined to be a threat only, not enough to warrant a charge of attempted murder.

Frederick Hollman was convicted on a charge of assault and battery before Justice John C. McConnell, Circuit Court Commissioner for Green Lake County in Dartford. It was reported Hollman served a sentence for the crime. 30 days in jail was the standard for assault in the county at the time.

Upon release, Hollman returned to his wife, much to everyone's astonishment.

Suspicion, resentment, and contention intensified in the Hollman household.

Even the birth of their second child, a son named Herman August Hollman, on July 16, 1891, provided no rainbow of hope for their marriage.

Six months later, on a cold January day in 1892, Frederick Hollman left his wife and two children and would never see them again.

Hollman did try to lure his wife back, but away from her safe haven in Green Lake County. A place where he was no longer welcomed.

"I tried to get my second wife back to live with me," Hollman once said about their estrangement. "I wrote her, but she did not answer. I wanted her to come where I was working, but she would not, and I gave up on trying."

Frederick Hollman briefly stayed with his brother in Ripon, then moved on.

He reportedly began a life on the lookout. Frederick feared Augusta would have him arrested and put back in jail, this time for abandonment. He began adopting assumed names as to conceal his true identity.

Frederick Hollman feared the past, but his greatest nightmare was on the pathway ahead.

Shunned and driven out by his community, Frederick Hollman became a transient working under several assumed names. He adopted "nomadic habits" and reportedly never worked at any one job for very long.

"I hardly ever worked more than a few days in one place," Hollman once admitted.

He also rarely resided at one location for very long, either.

A record of where Frederick Hollman went and what he did after leaving his family over the next four years mainly comes from his own recollections published in newspapers later. In many instances precise years are undetermined, and the first two years as a loner are virtually undocumented.

While details are scant, what is clear is that during this period Hollman began maintaining a presence in both Wisconsin and Illinois.

As a loner, Hollman continued to find employment as a farm hand and routinely took any type of work available. He was employed as sewing machine agent at one time and in 1894 worked at the Grant Marble Company in Milwaukee. He found work in Waukegan, Illinois and relocated to Chenoa shortly thereafter, establishing residency in the state.

In 1894, Frederick Hollman worked for farmer 55-year-old farmer Anton Sha in Danville City, in Vermilion County, Illinois. Next he was employed for a couple of weeks by farmer William L. Jacobs in Gibson City, where Hollman ran into some indiscretion.

"I had some trouble when I worked there, but I behaved like a gentleman," Hollman later recalled, in a defensive posture. "And I can prove it."

What went down at the Jacobs farmhouse remains unclear.

In April that year Hollman worked for William Yeagle near the village of Arrowsmith in McLean County, Illinois, next heading to nearby Bloomington for work. He was employed on the farms of William Carner and John Knight during the year, as well.

Hollman next found work as a brick layer that spring with August Misch, a mason. Hollman had worked previously as a brick layer, first entering the trade in Grand Haven a decade earlier. Misch paid him $1.75 per day's work, a fair sum in the day.

After working a few weeks for Misch, Hollman went back to Waukegan, Illinois where he had worked at various farms as a corn husker. He then sought work at locations northwest of Milwaukee, in northern Wisconsin in Randolph in Dodge County.

Hollman returned to Illinois in September 1895 and returned to the village of Arrowsmith working for farmer Dell Curtis.

Next he headed up to Dearborn, Michigan for eight days work, then returned to Illinois where he briefly stayed in Bloomington. He was in Gilman by November 1895 and stayed there four to five weeks at a farmhouse. Hollman next went to the residence of Henry Hart and then stayed two nights at the residence of Albert Lenz, where he worked for two days around Christmas.

At the beginning of 1896, Frederick Hollman took up residence for three months at a boarding house owned by John L. Maroney in Bloomington.

Maroney, born in 1866, was a businessman and a native of Bloomington. Hollman was employed as a handyman at the boarding house as well as being a boarder.

One newspaper reported that Hollman lived in Bloomington for "a few years," however, a "few years" was likely a "few months" at a time over a period of a few years. The Illinois Central railway had a major stop in Bloomington, from which he often traveled back and forth to Kenosha, Wisconsin finding work at the shipping port.

Hollman worked for six weeks chopping wood for John Brandt in Sullivant Township, Illinois in the early spring of 1896, then was hired by area farmer John Thompson until the end of May.

Hollman claimed he left Illinois around June 1 or 2, 1896 and headed by train back to Wisconsin to work that summer.

In the summer of 1896, Hollman stated he lived for one month at the home of Henry Lang, a 48-year-old farmer. Lang owned a farmhouse in Pleasant Prairie, Wisconsin and lived with his 44-year-old wife Henrietta, and two orphaned nephews, Jacob and Henry Lang.

Frederick Hollman had been using assumed names since the day he abandoned his wife and two children. Many he worked for knew him as Fred Hartman, Hallman, or Hoetman. Another assumed name he used was Fred Lang, no doubt due to his association with this family.

There is evidence Hollman was using the name Fred Lang a year earlier in 1895, an indication he had worked for and perhaps stayed with Henry Lange and his family before.

Hollman once said that he used false names because he feared Augusta "might try to find him." There is no evidence Hollman ever paid any support to Augusta for their two children after leaving them and he was concerned authorities would arrest him and return him to jail, this time for abandonment.

What transpired by the fall of 1896 was not a timeline of events Hollman would substantiate to any degree of credibility. In fact, from early June to the first days of December, his account of where he had been and what he did possessed some truth, some half-truths, and outright lies.

On December 6, Hollman would be in the Ford County, Illinois jail, charged with murder.

The final place Hollman admitted that he worked at before his arrested was at the Forman farm in Bloomington the first part of October 1896. He claimed by the end of that month he had returned to Milwaukee where he shucked corn. Hollman's final stint as a sailor occurred that fall as third wheelman on the steamer City of Milwaukee.

One location Frederick Hollman never mentioned having been during his years as a loner was the state of Pennsylvania. According to newspaper reports published in May 1897, during 1895 Hollman was working as a farm hand living at farmhouse near Hanover, Pennsylvania.

People who met him there said he went by the name Fred Lang. He told several people that he was married and had fathered "several children," but left Wisconsin "deserting his family." One of Hollman's Hanover neighbors said that he gathered the man's wife and children "were not adverse to his absence."

During his time there it was said Hollman mostly kept to himself. Residents reported observing him fishing a lot that summer. But the move to Pennsylvania had proved to be unfruitful as work was scarce. One account noted Hollman once sold silverware on the side to earn extra money.

Hollman departed the area in November soon after a woman was found dead of an assumed suicide. Suspicion concerning the death would surface with authorities until 17 months later.

As a loner, Hollman would only occasionally talk with people about the family he left behind in Wisconsin without revealing much detail.

According to various newspaper interviews with people who crossed his path, Hollman rarely spoke of his second daughter Minnie. He mentioned his son Herman frequently, but usually not by name. One example from 1896, while living near Gibson City, Illinois, he told a neighbor that he "had a six-year-old boy in Wisconsin."

People in the German communities where Hollman lived and worked found him peculiar in nature. Many had expressed fear of the man and with good reason. According to one published report, Hollman was a "woman hater" and had established quite a reputation for it. Hollman often shot off his mouth spewing vile comments about females.

"He has been heard frequently to remark that 'this woman or that woman' ought to be killed," The Chicago Tribune reported.

And Hollman badmouthed his wife Augusta every chance he got. By 1895 his hatred for his wife had manifested into an alarming threat to all women, and unknown to everyone, a killer was now on the prowl.

PART 2

A Trail of Madness and Murder

In 1896, corpses of German women began to turn up wherever Frederick Hollman had been. It wasn't until the third victim in the fall of that year that authorities from Wisconsin to Illinois began to focus suspicion on Hollman. The killing spree would not end until December 6, 1896 when he was apprehended and arrested.

One newspaper reported that the accused man's work "rivaled Jack the Ripper." Many other newspapers compared Hollman to H. H. Holmes.

H. H. Homes, born Herman Webster Mudgett, is commonly referred to as the first (documented) serial killer in America the modern sense of the term. He confessed to 27 murders, four of which were confirmed. Holmes was executed on May 7, 1896 for his crimes.

While Hollman had committed many assaults on women since 1890, including his own wife Augusta, he was accused of as many as six murders and eight attempted murders by 1896. His true number of victims may never be known.

Investigators in several states were reopening unsolved murder cases in areas where Hollman had lived or worked long after his trial. Of the six murders attributed to him, only five were discovered during his lifetime.

Hollman frequently traveled by rail from Bloomington, Illinois to Kenosha County, Wisconsin then back again to find work.

Kenosha County and the surrounding area, which included Pleasant Prairie, provided rail stops for the Chicago Northwestern, the Kenosha-Harvard line, and the CSMP&P Chicago-Milwaukee main line.

The Gibson City Courier reported in their December 10, 1896 edition that the correlation between the five murders attributed to Hollman was that "he was in the vicinity" on the day of each killing.

Other similarities or coincidences included the victims were "all were German women," all hung with cord around their necks attached to door knobs or bed posts (displayed) "in positions that precluding the idea of suicide."

Of these women, only one, Bertha Hilgendorf, did not have the trademark cord found around her neck.

The five murders attached to Frederick Hollman all occurred within six months, three in Illinois, two in Wisconsin.

The first murder attributed to Frederick Hollman occurred on the evening of June 13, 1896 when 60-year-old housewife Grethe Seifkin was found dead in the bedroom of her home near Melvin, Illinois. Her lifeless body was discovered by her second husband, Mathias Seifkin, age 45, who came in after his work on their farm.

Grethe Seifkin had been strangled to death then hung from a doorknob in the bedroom. Her head was suspended about a foot from the floor. Authorities discovered bruising on the woman's neck consistent with having been choked or strangled, but ruled the death a suicide.

"Lying on her bed she tied a rope to the knob of the bedroom door, and making a loose slip knot, slipped it over her head," the Gibson City Courier reported. "She then rolled off the bed and the rope strangled her to death."

Mathias Seifkin cut the cord from his wife's neck and went to tell a neighbor, Benjamin (Heinrichs) Hendricks. The neighbor advised him to inform Grethe's 25-year-old son, Anton Wolken, who lived only a few miles away.

Grethe Seifkin, born in Germany in 1836, immigrated to America with her five children settling in Iroquois County after the death of her first husband, Henry Wolken. She married Mathias Seifkin in Ford County on June 26, 1892.

When her son Anton arrived at the Seifkin farmhouse with his step-father, the Gibson City Courier described their reaction to her apparent suicide as "brutal indifference." The two were so disgusted by her apparent suicide that they left her body in the home overnight.

Mathias Seifkin stayed the night at the home of Wolken and they did not inform authorities about the death until the next day, Sunday morning.

That morning, Mathias Seikin notified 59-year-old Melvin Justice of the Peace John M. Thompson, who appointed a jury of six and held an inquest at the farmhouse that afternoon.

The grand jury foreman was John Iehl, a 57-year-old banker.

It was concluded the woman "came to her death by her own hand."

Mathias Seifkin and Anton Wolken were present at the inquest and it was reported the two "displayed the lack of feeling that characterized their conduct on the previous night."

Mathias declared he was too poor to pay for the cost of burying his wife, and her son Anton refused to bear the expense. Thus, Justice Thompson ordered a coffin at the expense of the county and Grethe Seifkin's remains were buried in the pauper section of Melvin Cemetery.

When she departed Germany in 1889, Grethe Seifkin had sold the little homestead which she owned with her first husband and divided the proceeds between her children. It was reported that after doing that Grethe Seifkin felt "slighted and neglected" by her children and had become feeble. Authorities believed this contributed to the theory she had taken her own life.

It was reported Frederick Hollman had at one time worked for Mathias and Grethe Seifkin and on the day of Grethe's death, Hollman was working as a farm hand for Seifkin neighbors Henry John and Sophia (Heinrichs) Hendricks.

Hollman would later acknowledge he "had passed by the Seifkin house" a day or two before the murder and admitted he had spoken to the woman. Hollman stated he mistook Grethe Seifkin for a neighbor, "Mrs. Hendrix," who he said he knew.

It was reported at the time of the murder, neighbors of Seifkin had seen Hollman with "scratches on his face," but the injuries "excited no suspicion."

Hollman also reportedly spoke with some curiosity seekers who had gathered outside the Seifkin farmhouse and "alleged that her husband had killed her."

Hollman later changed his story, removing himself from the crime scene by claiming he was in Chenoa, nearly 30 miles away when the murder took place.

The "Mrs. Hendrix" Hollman said he mistook Grethe Seifkin for was Sophia Hendricks, the wife of farmer Henry John Hendricks.

It is possible Sophia Hendricks was Hollman's intended target, but the opportunity never presented itself. Six months later, to the surprise of her family, the death of Grethe Seifkin was reclassified as a homicide.

Kevin Collier

The second murder attributed to Frederick Hollman was that of 56-year-old Bertha Hilgendorf, whose body was discovered on July 4, 1896 in a milk house at her 240 acre farm residence in Pleasant Prairie, three miles west of Kenosha, Wisconsin.

Born Bertha Albertine Krueger in Pommern, Germany in 1841, she married August Wilhelm Hilgendorf on September 19, 1864 in Theresa, Wisconsin. They had three sons, William, Bernhard and Oscar. William married in 1886 and lived on his own, while brothers Bernhard and Oscar lived with their parents.

The day of Bertha Hilgendorf's murder her husband August was a few miles away celebrating the Fourth of July with friends. He had left his wife and two sons at home around 8:00 that morning.

August Hilgendorf, age 61, was a well-known Milwaukee saloon keeper of 20 years who also owned a grocery store in that city.

The Milwaukee Journal described him as "rather well-to-do, but somewhat addicted to alcohol." Another newspaper called August Hilgendorf "a habitual drinker."

August Hilgendorf's adult sons, Bernhard and Oscar, found their father drunk in Kenosha on July 4 shortly after noon and brought him home. One newspaper described Hilgendorf's condition as "gloriously drunk." Dropping him off, the sons then departed.

Soon August discovered his wife's lifeless body in a milk house on the property, which was located 15 yards from the dwelling.

Bertha Hilgendorf had been murdered with a rusty corn cutter, which was discovered at her side. Her throat was slashed, skull crushed and the upper part of her body had been stripped of clothing displaying bruising on each of her sides. There was also significant bruising on both of her arms, indicative of defensive wounds, indicating she had fought her attacker.

August Hilgendorf made no effort to alert neighbors or authorities and waited for his sons to return home.

When August's sons arrived home about 6:30 p.m., their father suggested that Bernhard should "look in the milk room and see what is there."

Once seeing his mother's mutilated body, Bernhard ran over to a neighbor's home and sought help from 21-year-old William Thomey. Once at the Hilgendorf residence, Thomey witnessed a seemingly unconcerned August Hilgendorf milking the cows. Thomey then drove Bernhard to Kenosha where they notified Sheriff Samuel B. Cropley about the death.

Police arrived at the scene early that evening. An inquest jury was formed at the location and the coroner estimated Bertha Hilgendorf had been dead for "more than three hours."

Suspicion fell upon August Hilgendorf.

His shirt sleeves and shoes were smeared with a considerable amount of blood and investigators noticed "some efforts" had apparently been made to clean the shirt.

Remnants of supper were visible on the kitchen table, showing August Hilgendorf had eaten while his wife's corpse remained in the milk house. He had not even bothered to cover his wife's half-nude body with a sheet.

August Hilgendorf told authorities the blood on his garments were transferred onto him when he attempted to lift his wife's body to carry her into the house. Due to his drunken stupor, he had left her in the milk house.

Sheriff Samuel Cropley had August change his clothing and took the bloody garments into his possession as evidence.

Strangely, August Hilgendorf's body showed no significant signs of markings or wounds that would have resulted from a violent struggle with his wife.

Due to circumstantial evidence, authorities arrested August Hilgendorf and son Bernhard and took them into custody. August was charged with murder and jailed but after questioning Bernhard was soon released.

Initial reports concerning the death pointed to transients as likely suspects.

A report in the Stevens Point Journal stated in a headline Bertha Hilgendorf was "Probably killed by a tramp." The newspaper explained, "Both he and a son, who found the murdered woman are under arrest, but many attribute the crime to tramps."

According to the Milwaukee Journal, August Hilgendorf at the time authorities arrived at the scene "tried to get up a theory of suicide" to explain the death of his wife. But police and the coroner ruled the evidence supported the cause of death to be murder.

Bertha Albertine Hilgendorf was laid to rest in Union Cemetery, Milwaukee, Wisconsin on July 6, 1896 beside two sons and two daughters who had died in their youth.

August Hilgendorf was placed on trial for the murder of his wife.

Sons Bernard and Oscar testified at trial and revealed that their mother and father quarreled a great deal. The arguments concerned property Bertha Hilgendorf owned that her husband wanted her to sell to pay off debts on their farm.

August Hilgendorf took the witness stand and reportedly make "a general denial of all charges against him." Although the case was entirely circumstantial, the property owned by Bertha Hilgendorf, and value of it, became a motive for murder.

August Hilgendorf was convicted of first degree murder on September 23, 1896 and sentenced to life at the Waupun Correctional Institution.

Frederick Hollman, at the time of Bertha Hilgendorf's death, was employed cutting corn for a farmer who lived only one mile from the Hilgendorf residence. Hollman left town the day after the murder but not before shooting off his mouth telling neighbors near the scene that "August Hilgendorf had killed his wife."

Hollman later became a suspect in this killing when he revealed details of the method of the murder not released to the press by authorities. It was information only the killer would know.

Coincidently, the September 23, 1896 edition of The Milwaukee Journal published two news items that day that would later connect to Frederick Hollman.

On page two of that day's edition, an article with the headline "Killed his wife" appeared announcing the jury had convicted August Hilgendorf for murder of his wife. On page 9, a news brief appeared concerning the death of a woman named Anna Catherine Mohr.

Police suspected Mohr had been killed during the commission of a robbery.

While the murder of Hilgendorf and Mohr occurred eleven weeks apart, the locations of the deaths, Pleasant Prairie and Somers respectively, were as little as seven miles apart.

Within weeks, authorities were on the trail of a "Fred Lang" as the primary suspect in this murder. It was an assumed name Frederick Hollman had been using that summer.

The third murder attributed to Frederick Hollman was that of Anna Catherine Mohr on September 20, 1896 in the town of Somers, Wisconsin, a few miles west of Kenosha. Mohr was a widow who lived with her 37-year-old bachelor son Andrew. Anna's husband, Jacob, had passed away in 1875.

The 73-year-old woman had been strangled then hung from a door knob using binding cord and $25 was missing from a wooden box, money the victim had earned the previous day from the sale of a cow.

Survivors included another son, Christian, and a daughter, Mary (Mohr) Bucher, both married, who lived in Racine, as well as a sister of Mrs. Mohr, Agnes (Mohr) Kerner.

According to reports, Frederick Hollman was working in the neighborhood at the time under the name of Fred Lang. He had approached the Mohr residence the end of August or first week of September and had spoken to Andrew Mohr inquiring about work for hire. Andrew turned him away, as there was none.

The day of the murder, Andrew Mohr had left his mother unattended at home when he departed for Kenosha before noon to purchase groceries and other goods. He discovered her body about 2:00 that afternoon when he returned home.

Andrew discovered his mother's body suspended by the neck two inches off the floor outside of his bedroom using a cord fastened to the knob of the door of the room.

Authorities did not respond until the following day. That evening it was believed Anna Catherine Mohr had taken her own life, perhaps in response to having heart disease.

Upon further investigation into the death by Sheriff Samuel B. Cropley and an inquest jury, it was determined the woman had been murdered. Doctor Gustav Windesheim of Kenosha, who thoroughly examined Mrs. Mohr's body after the coroner, agreed, and classified the death as a murder.

Inside Mohr's home, the wooden box that contained the $25 reported to be missing had been opened using an ax, likely by an intruder. Also, the pockets in Mrs. Mohr's dress were discovered to have been turned inside out.

Strangely, on the kitchen table an amount of sugar granules were found. Sugar was something Andrew said his mother never used.

It would be learned later that days prior to Anna Catherine Mohr's death Frederick Hollman had approached neighbors of the Mohrs and inquired "if the old woman lived alone" with her son.

Andrew Mohr would later identify Frederick Hollman from a photograph circulated by authorities as being the "Fred Lang" he had met at the front door of his mother's home seeking work.

At the time of Anna Catherine Mohr's murder Frederick Hollman was wanted by authorities in Pleasant Prairie, Wisconsin on a charge of attempted assault on 25-year-old Mary Schram. Mary Schram and her husband, Daniel, were immigrants from Austria and had two children.

A warrant had been issued for the arrest of a "Fred Lang" a few weeks before the Mohr killing.

Hollman fled the state after Mohr's death and next popped up in the little town of Holder, just east of Bloomington in McLean County, Illinois.

There he became acquainted with John Sieh, who was a farmer. Sieh hired Hollman to pick corn and act as a farm hand.

When John Sieh was away at town, Hollman entered his home where his wife Eliza was left unattended. Hollman reportedly made improper proposals to the 38-year-old housewife, which she rejected. This enraged Hollman. The intruder then attacked Eliza, beating and choking her "into insensibility."

In the Sieh case, authorities wanted to issue an arrest warrant but it was unclear whom they were looking for. Unknown to Bloomington authorities, a few weeks after the incident involving Eliza Sieh, the city of Waukegan, Illinois would "have their man."

In early November, Hollman was arrested in Waukegan after he was discovered hiding under a woman's bed inside of her home.

Hollman was taken into custody by 40-year-old Thomas Tyrall, who was the Marshall of Lake County. Tyrall resided in Waukegan with his wife Anna and their eight children.

During questioning, Hollman gave authorities no explanation as to why he was inside of the residence.

Tyrall lodged Hollman in the Waukegan jail on a charge of breaking and entering and released the prisoner after a few days. At the time, Waukegan authorities had no idea Hollman was wanted in Bloomington, Illinois.

Hollman would later say this brush with the law took all his money, approximately $40.

Upon his release, Hollman headed back to Ford County, Illinois where in Gibson City he nearly strangled 31-year-old Mary Elizabeth Schertz to death. Schertz' brother Peter rescued her from the attacker who vanished before authorities arrived. Schertz recovered.

The assailant would later be identified as Hollman.

The fourth murder attributed to Frederick Hollman was Caroline (Carrie) Amanda Lenz, 22-years-old, who resided with her husband in the city of Gilman, Iroquois County, a few miles north of Danforth.

Her husband, 30-year-old farmer Albert Lenz, left to see a oilman early on Thanksgiving Day, November 26, 1896. His wife, whom all called Carrie, remained at home with their two children, Charles and Florence. Charles was nearly age two, Florence was no more than 6 months.

Carrie Lenz was busy preparing to iron laundry and had placed pies in the oven to bake when Hollman reportedly knocked at the front door. Lenz likely bore no suspicion, allowing the man inside, as she knew Frederick Hollman. He had been employed by Albert Lenz the previous year in Autumn and was recognized upon his return to the neighborhood.

Around 9:00 a.m., Julius Lenz, a brother-in-law, stopped by for a visit and discovered the lifeless body of Carrie Lenz.

She had been beaten and was found tied by the neck to a door knob using binding twine. Her head was said to have been suspended several inches above the floor.

An initial determination of suicide was quickly ruled out.

Carrie Lenz had scratches on her neck and bruises on one shoulder and her side. The theory was that she had been attacked from behind.

The cord found around the neck of Carrie Lenz was said to have been used to tie up Charles' pet dog. It was discovered the bundle of rope it had come from had 16 feet or more missing.

Charles and Florence, who were present at the time of their mother's murder, were likely unaware of what had taken place. The Gilman Star newspaper reported the children were "too young to give any clue to the mystery."

Within days, authorities suspected Hollman was connected to the death when a small gold watch with case and a smaller silver (or nickel) watch owned by Carrie Lenz were seen in his possession shortly after the murder.

According to Hollman, he claimed he stayed the evening of November 26 at the boarding house owned by John L. Maroney in Bloomington. Hollman had lived there in the past and was once an employee of Maroney.

"He (Hollman) asked me if I wanted to buy a watch," Maroney later said. "The one he had (showed me) was a ladies watch, about the size of a (silver) dollar."

According to reports, apparently one the dead woman's watches, the "silver" one, was said to have been in the possession of 67-year-old widow Eliza C. Cambell, a lady Hollman admired in Bloomington.

Days after the murder, Hollman had worked for Meent R. Meents in the nearby town of Ashkum, approximately 9 miles north of Gilman.

Meents, a 46-year-old German immigrant who settled in Illinois in 1869, was a senior partner in the firm of M. R. Meents & Sons, bankers and dealers in grain, lumber, coal and seeds in the towns of Ashkum and Clifton.

While employed there Hollman brought a piece of the cord or rope to use at Meents' farm.

While the cord found around Carrie Lenz's neck had been destroyed, a small piece was cut off before the inquest and kept by Samuel Stone, a grand jury member. Stone was a 54-year-old horse doctor from Danforth.

The rope Hollman had used at the Meents farm was reportedly an "identical match" to the rope reported missing from the Lenz farm and found around the victim's neck.

Hollman was identified by three individuals as being seen near the Lenz home the morning of the murder. He was also identified by William Kerber, who had hired Hollman to farm a portion of the Lenz property a year earlier.

Kerber recognized Hollman upon his return to the area and others stated the suspect was "in the neighborhood about the time of the murder."

Police who had canvassed the area the morning Carrie Lenz was murdered discovered that the prior evening, less than one mile away from the murder scene, a man had tried to break into another house, but was unsuccessful.

Authorities questioned the woman at that home, who had been alone in the house that the time. She told authorities that the locks on the home were secure and "after working for two hours" to break in, "the man went away."

The woman's husband returned home from at trip at 2:00 that morning and she informed him of the would-be intruder. The press reported the woman and her husband "thought it was a wandering tramp."

In short order, everyone in the area would suspect the "tramp" attempting the home break-in had been Frederick Hollman.

Kevin Collier

The fifth and final murder victim attributed to Frederick Hollman was Wiebke Geddes, the 28-year-old wife of Fred Geddes, resident tenants on the John Stroh farm located near the town of Sibley about eight miles northwest of Gibson City in Ford County, Illinois.

Land owner John Fred Stroh, age 51, was a successful farmer who came to the United States from Weddingstedt Holstein, Germany with his wife Margaret in 1873.

Fred Geddes, a 30-year-old employee of John Stroh, had departed the house between 4:30-5:00 on the cold Wednesday morning of December 2, 1896 to husk feed corn. He left his wife asleep at the home with their daughter Elizabeth.

Between 8:30-9:00 a.m., neighbor Michael Voss, who was fixing a gate on a fence near the residence, went to the Geddes house for the purpose of warming his hands.

When no one came to the door, Voss went inside where he discovered the stiff, cold body of Wiebke Geddes in the southwest corner of the bedroom. She was clad in only an under vest. Around her neck was binding twine attached to the door knob of an adjacent room.

The residence appeared to be ransacked. Slats from the bed were scattered about and some dresser drawers had been left open.

"It (the binding twine) was doubled and a noose made at the end," the Chatsworth Plaindealer newspaper reported. "The loose ends were wound around, but not tied to, the doorknob."

Evidence showed Wiebke Geddes had engaged in a struggle with her killer.

Geddes' fingernails bore traces of blood and human flesh that were undoubtedly from her assailant. Her body was badly bruised having suffered a beating with a spading fork and said to have been "scratched from head to foot."

A portion of her skull, the size of a silver dollar, had been caved in. It was also reported that one of the victim's legs had been broken.

Most alarmingly, the Geddes' 6-year-old handicapped daughter, Elizabeth, was found crying in the room. She had been present at the time of her mother's murder and was said to have been in bed sleeping with her mother when the intruder appeared.

One report stated Elizabeth Geddes was seated in the middle of the broken down bed, holding a pair of scissors in her hand and sobbing. It was revealed Elizabeth had used the scissors to cut some of the twine that was attached to her mother's neck in an attempt to release her.

"I called to mama," Elizabeth told investigators. "But she didn't speak. I took the shears and cut the string, but she still didn't speak."

Evidence showed the little girl, described as being a "cripple since birth" and who wore a custom "corset" due to a weak spine, had been assaulted and "showed signs" of being strangled.

"Marks on the neck of the little girl showed that she had been choked," the Chicago Tribune reported. The newspaper said the act by the assailant was either to "render the girl unconscious" or that she had been "left for dead."

Neighbor Michael Voss, upon discovering Wiebke Geddes' body, took Elizabeth from the house and brought her to his residence to remain in the care of his wife, Johanna.

He informed Johanna and their children of what he had discovered at the Geddes residence. Voss then sent his youngest daughter, Mary, to the main farmhouse to notify owner John Stroh that "Mrs. Geddes was dead."

John Stroh Sr. sent his son John out into the cornfield to fetch the dead woman's husband. Stroh instructed his son to tell Fred Geddes only that his wife "was sick" and to see his father regarding the matter. John Stroh Sr. wanted Geddes to get the information of his wife's murder from him, not the boy.

Once receiving the message, Geddes informed the boy he would return to the farmhouse after finishing his load.

At about noon, Fred Geddes completed his work and came in where John Stroh Sr. informed him of the murder.

Geddes initially laughed and refused to believe that his wife had been murdered.

"You're joking with me," he reportedly said.

John Stroh Sr. and others at the farm escorted Fred Geddes to the scene at the home, and upon seeing his wife's body, Geddes broke down and cried. He also declared that he had no idea what had happened.

But suspicion upon him was already brewing.

Some workers on the farm thought Fred Geddes' initial behavior was cavalier. He had not come in from the field when Stroh's son had informed him his wife was "sick," and had laughed at the news she was dead.

What acquaintances did not know was that Wiebke Geddes was prone to routine headaches that left her feeling ill. She was frequently "sick," but not in a life threatening in manner.

The Geddes' daughter, Elizabeth, now in the care of Mrs. Voss, had been telling the woman she called "Aunt Johanna" about what had happened at the house.

Elizabeth had told Johanna Voss that "my bad papa done it" and described a terrible struggle between her father and mother just prior to the death. Elizabeth added her father had choked her but she had crawled under the bed to hide.

A messenger bearing the news of the murder was sent to Gibson City and around 3:00 that afternoon to alert authorities.

Constable Ira Gilmore, a party of citizens, coroner William A. Hutchison and assistant Owen Kirk arrived at the murder scene. Hutchison, age 46, quickly impaneled a jury.

Truman D. Spaulding, a 58-year-old lumber merchant, was selected as foreman of the inquest jury. He was joined by Fred W. Beardsley, a 65-year-old farmer, property owner John Stroh, Henry Heinrichs, a 56-year-old farmer, Arthur E. Wood, a 34-year old old grain buyer and August Neish.

An inquiry commenced and an investigation of the premises was conducted at once.

Fred Geddes was the first person questioned by the men.

He testified he had not been home at the time of the murder and recalled his schedule that morning. He relayed that he and his wife always "lived harmoniously" and protested the inquiry insisting that he was "innocent of the crime."

When Elizabeth Geddes was questioned as to who had committed the deed, she replied, "Papa came back after he went away and jumped on mama and swore at her, and killed her."

She repeated what she had told Johanna Voss and added that her father hung her mother from the door knob. Elizabeth also said that her mother had named the intruder upon his entry. She said her mother had asked, "Fred, Fred, is that you?"

Outdoors, a search was conducted using bloodhounds that uncovered a pair of bloody overalls and a work shirt belonging to Fred Geddes in a stack of hay on the farm near the home.

Indoors, the spading fork, which normally stood in the corner of the living room, was found under the bed. The fork had been borrowed from Michael Voss for the purpose of digging potatoes. It was concluded upon the examination of Wiebke Geddes' body that her death was caused by being struck in the head by the farming implement.

The jury returned a verdict charging Fred Geddes with the murder of his wife and recommended that he be bound over for trial without bail.

Fred Geddes was arrested by Constable Ira Gilmore at the scene and brought to Paxton around 8:00 that evening where he was lodged in the Ford County jail in the custody of Sheriff Benjamin Franklin Mason.

Word spread quickly concerning the murder of Wiebke Geddes and the arrest of her husband.

By coincidence, The Watseka Republican, located about 50 miles from Sibley, published news of the death of Carrie Lenz on the same day Wiebke Geddes was found dead.

Citizens became both fearful and outraged concerning the death of Wiebke Geddes.

Newspapers reported in the following days up to 300 men and boys marched outside of the Ford County jailhouse shouting, "We want Geddes!"

The initial outcry against Fred Geddes dissipated as talk began to circulate pointing to the actual perpetrator.

Many of Fred Geddes neighbors and closest friends did not believe he was guilty from the beginning, regardless of what his daughter had said.

The family of John Stroh relayed Fred Geddes had sat down for breakfast with them that morning and "he appeared as usual, showing no guilt or even excitement." They reported seeing no wounds on Mr. Geddes, as well.

On Thursday, December 3, Sheriff Mason began conducting an investigation to determine if his prisoner was indeed the murder. Fred Geddes had been strip searched while in jail and it was reported "not as much as a pin scratch was found on his person."

"There was not a scratch or bruise on his (Fred Geddes') body," one newspaper reported. "And, it was evident the woman left her mark on her assailant, whoever he was."

Things were not adding up.

Fred Geddes did not fit the profile of a murderer and neighbors and friends said he had cared for his "near-invalid wife" admirably.

And his daughter Elizabeth was changing her story as well.

She now said her father had gotten up early the morning of December 2 to light a lamp, dressed himself, then put out the light upon leaving the house. Elizabeth said, then "someone came into the room."

While canvassing the town of Sibley for witnesses, traces of information began to surface about a stranger in the area who had been "posing as a chicken buyer."

However, the discovery of Fred Geddes' bloody garments hidden in a straw stack could not be explained. Thus Geddes was held at the jail and not allowed to attend his wife's funeral.

Wiebke Geddes' funeral took place Friday, December 3 at St. John's Lutheran Church in Anchor Township, with burial at the church cemetery.

By Saturday morning, December 4, the Grand Jury met and decided the case against Geddes was so weak that they could no longer continue to hold him.

Charges were promptly dismissed and Fred Geddes was released.

A free man, Geddes, reunited with his daughter, did not return home. They moved into the house of Claus Johannson, a 38-year-old farmer and friend who lived with his wife Dora northeast of Elliott, about 6 miles east of Gibson City.

Fred and Wiebke Geddes, natives of Germany, had lived in the United States for only two years at the time of her murder.

PART 3

The Hunt for Hollman

On Saturday, the December 5, 1896 edition of the Chicago Tribune announced in an article that authorities had officially ruled out Fred Geddes as a suspect in the death of his wife. The newspaper reported lawmen in Gibson City were looking for a man who was "seen by the children of neighbors" and others running from the Geddes residence before dawn the day of the killing.

Investigators had ruled the initial testimony of 6-year-old Elizabeth Geddes, incriminating her father, was "unreliable."

"The woman was killed before daybreak and it is believed the child could not have distinguished between her father and any other man," the Chicago Tribune reported. "Geddes said he had gotten up and gone to the field before daybreak."

Fred Geddes had told authorities that a search he had conducted himself of his home the day of the murder, and subsequently after his release from jail, turned up several missing items.

Geddes revealed that a light-colored pocketbook owned by his wife containing some money and his Sollingen shaving razor were missing.

Geddes also stated, "a gold ring with my wife's name inside" was among missing items. The gold, engraved wedding band could have been misplaced inside the home at the time, and found sometime later.

By that Saturday, the same men who had comprised the Fred Geddes Grand Jury redirected their attention to a "tramp" or "stranger" many individuals had mentioned during the three day investigation of the dead woman's husband.

Authorities had received many tips from concerned citizens regarding a man "posing as a chicken buyer" and began tracking the movements of the stranger.

Margaret Voss, wife of Michael, told authorities a few days before the murder of neighbor Wiebke Geddes, a stranger posing as "a chicken buyer" had called at her home, then had been in the Geddes home.

The stranger was hungry and was invited in for something to eat. According to Margaret Voss, for three hours the stranger frightened Mrs. Geddes with "vile proposals." Voss recalled she encountered the scene when she stopped at the Geddes residence to pay a routine visit.

Geddes invited Voss in, and at her request, Voss stayed. Feeling uncomfortable, the stranger departed shortly thereafter.

Voss recalled Wiebke Geddes said the man's name was "Fred Hartman."

Authorities now theorized Fred Geddes' bloody garments found hidden in a straw stack on the property had been worn by this man, who somehow had stolen them from the house that day and worn them the morning of the murder.

Investigators suspected "Hartman" might have dressed in Fred Geddes' clothing as an illusion to trick the woman into thinking it was her husband thus allowing him inside the house. The theory was supported by Elizabeth Geddes, the dead woman's daughter, who had told authorities that her mother had asked, "Fred, Fred, is that you?" when the man came inside.

44-year-old farmer Chris Walters and his wife Katie recalled a man who worked for them on occasion had also talked about "buying chickens."

The man, who they knew as Fred Hartman, ate supper, played cards, drank whiskey and stayed overnight at their home on Monday, November 30.

Hartman told Chris and Katie Walters he planned to take the money he earned from husking corn over a month and "buy chickens with it." While there, Hartman had exhibited two ladies wrist watches. One was a gold, the other one silver, or nickel.

This encounter took place four days after the nearby slaying of Carrie Lenz and two days before the murder of Wiebke Geddes.

"Folks were so scared they kept their doors locked and loaded guns at hand," the Walters' daughter Rosa recalled.

With Fred Geddes in the clear, it meant his wife's killer was still at large. Pressure on authorities was paramount that weekend to quickly apprehend a suspect. It was their initial investigation of Fred Geddes had inadvertently put them on the trail of the actual killer.

A story similar to the Walters encounter also surfaced.

The man known as Fred Hartman had recently been a house guest of the Bushman family. John Bushman, a 41-year-old farmer, lived with his wife Mattie, age 39, and their five children two and a half miles west of Guthrie. The Bushmans were familiar with Hartman as he had worked for them cutting wood in February 1896.

Hartman had popped up at their door on November 28, two days after the murder of Carrie Lenz. He was looking for work. Hartman was hungry and his feet were blistered from walking so he was invited in.

Mattie gave him a bucket to soak his sore feet and the couple invited Hartman to stay overnight Saturday and Sunday.

During his stay with at the Bushman home, Hartman showed off a two women's watches and an engraved case to John and Mattie Bushman and their children. He bragged of owning "eighty acres of land" in Wisconsin, and had mentioned he was going to "buy up chickens" for a business venture that could potentially earn him a lot of money.

Hartman, however, was obviously destitute.

John Bushman suggested to Hartman he try to find work with farmer Henry (Hank) Selberg. Bushman worked for the man, and promised to put in a good word.

Hartman departed their residence Monday morning. November 30.

That afternoon, Kate Hanson, who lived 4 and a half miles southwest of Melvin encountered Hartman at her house. The man asked her where "Hank" Stuhmer lived as he wanted to go there to "shuck corn."

During their encounter, Hollman reportedly tried to sell Kate a ladies gold watch he said he had purchased in Chicago. The meeting occurred less than 48 hours before Wiebke Geddes was murdered.

Kate and her husband Claus were very good friends of the Geddes and had put them up in their house when they first came to America.

Hollman received directions o the Stuhmer farm, then departed.

On Tuesday, the day before Wiebke Geddes was murdered, Hartman had shown up at the homes of both Emma Schroeder and Mary Borchers looking for a place to stay the night. At the Borchers residence Mary's mother, Katherina Jensen, was home alone at the time and answered the door.

Hollman was refused an invitation at both locations.

It was learned the night before the murder of Wiebke Geddes someone had slept in the one-room Ashley schoolhouse near the Geddes home. On December 2, the day of the murder, a student by the name of Julius Heckens had arrived at the school around 8:00 that morning to start a fire in the wood stove. He discovered one already lit but near smolder, evidence someone had stayed there.

School teacher Lilian Johnson, upon her arrival moments later, noticed a key to the school building was missing and a tiny hand-held mirror she owned was nowhere to be found.

John and Minnie Stroh, the son and daughter of farm owner John Stroh, reported they had witnessed a man hurrying across the field on the property at about 6:00 a.m. the day of the Geddes murder. They stated the man was headed in the direction of the Ashley schoolhouse.

That afternoon, student Faye Preston discovered a wash basin hidden beneath the porch of the schoolhouse that appeared to have traces of blood on it.

Henry (Hank) Selberg, age 20, a neighbor of the Geddes who worked 170 acres at the John Zimmerman farm, said he also encountered the stranger early on the morning of the Geddes murder.

Selberg stated he and the man exchanged greetings on the road. Selberg told authorities he was "nervous of the man" as the stranger acted hurried and his face and chin were covered with blood.

The man asked Selberg about employment and wanted directions to the Stuhmer farm as he was looking for a place to stay.

The stranger said he knew Hank (Hans) Stuhmer and had crossed paths with his brother John. The two brothers lived at a farmhouse owned by their father, John (Johann) Stuhmer, a farmer in his mid-50s who had immigrated from Dilslad, Germany. The farmhouse was located a few miles east of the Geddes residence.

Coincidentally, John Stuhmer's wife Dora was the daughter of John Stroh, owner of the farm and residence where the Geddes family lived.

Selberg provided directions to the farmhouse as best he could, then the man left.

Hartman arrived at the Stuhmer farm around 11:30 a.m. and was hired to husk corn.

Harvey Bainter and his step-brother William Guise worked beside Hartman briefly that day. Both men noticed the man's face was badly scratched and swollen and he had complained of having a toothache.

Many others at the farm noticed the man's appearance as well, and imagined he'd been involved in a fist fight earlier that day.

William Guise had been in town late that morning and had heard of the death of Wiebke Geddes. In the field, he brought the subject up in front of Hartman. Guise and others noticed the man "hung his head" and "looked uncomfortable."

According to Hank Stuhmer, Hartman worked part of that day then abruptly departed that afternoon.

The evening of December 2, Hartman returned to the residence of John and Mattie Bushman again and was invited to stay the night. While there, the Hartman brought up the murder of Wiebke Geddes and seemed to know many details about it.

Hartman did not report for work the next day, December 3, at the Stuhmer farm.

On Friday morning, December 4, Hartman arrived back at the home of Claus and Kate Hanson. Kate, who was on the porch and home alone, let the man inside where he went on about the details in the murder of Wiebke Geddes.

While there, Hartman tried to sell her a gold woman's watch, but Hanson declined. He also showed her a shaving razor with the brand name "Sollingen" on it. She recalled the man "talked poorly of women" and seemed very "preoccupied" with the murder.

Claus Hanson encountered Hartman upon his return to work at the Stuhmer farm in a cornfield the afternoon of December 4. He noticed scratches on Hartman's face.

After returning home, Claus heard about the shaving razor his wife had been shown it is matched the description of Fred Geddes' stolen razor. Claus had actually used the razor once when the Geddes stayed with them upon arriving in America.

All of the witnesses authorities interviewed described the suspect's garments precisely the same, that he was "wearing a scotch cap and a gray overcoat."

Many reported the man appeared to have suffered from "wounds from a struggle." The suspect had also become outspoken proclaiming the guilt of Fred Geddes in the death of his wife. This drew more attention to Hartman.

Matthew Kerber, employed at the Stuhmer farm, recalled Hartman was "acting queerly" upon his return to work that Friday. 42-year-old Kerber had noticed "reddish-brown" scratches on man's face and said Hartman claimed he received the scratches when making his way through a hedge. Hartman also offered no explanation for his two-day absence.

That Friday, Hartman made arrangements to reside at the Stuhmer farmhouse as a boarder and paid for an upstairs bedroom. He would remain there for the weekend.

While there, members of the Stuhmer family reported Hartman had displayed a man's shaving razor, and a two women's watches, one gold and one silver.

Hartman shared the bedroom with another man and slept on a simple bed tick, essentially a wooden frame containing a sack stuffed with corn husks, which served as a mattress.

Hartman took his meals at the Stuhmer farmhouse sitting down to eat in the company of his coworkers. According to those fellow diners, Hartman often talked about his spite for women.

According to Hank Stuhmer, Hartman seemed "to have an antipathy" toward women. He spoke of females with hostility with fixed opposition and disgust.

Stuhmer would later say he became suspicious of Hartman as early on as Friday, December 4, when he first boarded at the farmhouse. In a conversation Stuhmer had with the Hartman about the murder of Wiebke Geddes, he said the man stated women "ought to be killed," and named one.

The woman's name was Anna Defries, the wife of neighboring farmer Herman Defries. Stuhmer said Hartman told him Defries, whom he saw a mean-spirited, deserved to be dead.

The pieces were coming together quickly over the weekend of December 5-6.

The man police were looking for was working and staying at the Stuhmer farm. Authorities received confirmation when a messenger from the Stuhmer farm appeared at the Sheriff's office on Sunday, December 6, informing them, "we have your man."

Kevin Collier

After authorities were tipped off that the man suspected of murdering Wiebke Geddes was at the Stuhmer farmhouse, a telephone call was placed there to confirm the person of interest was still on the property.

Frederick Hollman, known by all there under a assumed name, Fred Hartman, had taken a walk early that day, but was still at the residence. A silent and clandestine vigil quickly organized within the house and Hank Stuhmer and August Myer kept a watchful eye on Frederick Hollman that afternoon.

Margaret Voss was summoned to the Stuhmer farmhouse to identify the suspect. She spied a glance at Hollman and confirmed this was the man who had been at the Geddes residence posing as "a chicken buyer," and at her home, as well.

Messengers were sent to neighbors and an inconspicuous gathering soon formed to join in the watch.

John Stroh, Matthew Kerber, Fred Geddes, Albert Lenz, Albert Selburg, Henry Heckens (an older brother to Julius) and two of Matthew Garber's sons showed up at the Stuhmer farm. They kept an eye out all afternoon to ensure Frederick Hollman would not flee. Hollman, seeming unaware of gathering and not feeling well do to a toothache, retired early to his room just after sunset.

A warrant was obtained and Constable Ira Gilmore who was accompanied by an armed posse from Gibson City. They moved onto the property by 8:00 that evening. At the time authorities arrived at the farmhouse, as many as "twenty to thirty men" had gathered at the location to ensure the suspect did not escape.

Gilmore and his posse climbed the stairs and Frederick Hollman was awakened, riled from his bed and placed under arrest. Hollman was not asleep at all, but hiding under a sheet pretending he was, it was reported.

Frederick Hollman identified himself as "Fred Hartman" to Constable Gilmore. Reportedly, he showed no emotion whatsoever while being held, even though it was said "he knew" he had become the prime suspect in the murder of Wiebke Geddes.

At that moment of his arrest a search was conducted for evidence and interviews were taken at the farmhouse. Hollman showed no physical resistance but protested he "was innocent" of any crime.

A search was conducted of luggage and a trunk owned by the suspect and Hollman was frisked and his person searched.

Constable Gilmore reportedly found in Hollman's possession a woman's pocket book, which had contained five dollars in German bills, coins and a silver watch with a chain attached.

There is no mention in any reports of an engraved, gold wedding ring, owned by Wiebke Geddes, found in Hollman's possession. The husband of the murdered woman, Fred Geddes, had told authorities it was missing from the home.

Constable Gilmore found the key to the nearby Ashley schoolhouse in Hollman's pocket. He also found the tiny hand mirror owned by school teacher Lilian Johnson.

When questioned, Frederick Hollman denied staying inside of the schoolhouse and said the day in question he was in transit coming from Waukegan to Joliet then from Joliet to Bloomington via train.

When Hollman's shirt was removed, a long bruise was discovered on his back. It would prove to match the length and configuration of the spading fork found in the Geddes home, which authorities claimed was the murder weapon.

It was later determined Wiebke Geddes had likely picked up the spading fork to fend off her attacker, and he had taken it from her using it to kill her.

Hollman dismissed the scratches on his face as having anything to do with "a struggle." He explained they were received when "crawling through a hedge."

A witness or two interviewed earlier by authorities had claimed they encountered Hollman after the murder of Wiebke Geddes "making his is way through a hedge."

Hollman also had a bruise on his forehead as if he had been struck. His lip was also bruised, and two teeth were ulcerated giving the appearance someone had punched him in the mouth.

Constable Gilmore and the posse escorted Hollman to the Ford County jail that Sunday evening where he was lodged overnight.

On Monday morning, December 7, Frederick Hollman was brought before Justice of the Peace Jacob W. Preston for preliminary examination in Gibson City. Present at the examination was Samuel Johnson, a city Marshall of Gibson City and 35-year-old Illinois State Attorney Abraham Lincoln Phillips, who would be prosecuting the Wiebke Geddes murder case.

Also present was Attorney Columbus S. Schneider, a 28-year-old lawyer who had practiced less than 2 years. Columbus Schneider and his older brother, Rudolph L Schneider, were members of the Ford County Bar Association and operated the firm of Schneider & Schneider in 1895. Schneider volunteered to represent Frederick Hollman at trial.

Columbus Schneider, his wife Mattie, and their two daughters, Maureen and Portia, made their home in Gibson City. Schneider was born in Columbus, Ohio, but his parents were immigrants from Germany. He often was assigned criminal cases involving defendants of Germany ancestry and language.

Hollman had no money to hire an attorney, so Schneider suggested they would find ways to raise funds for his defense. Schneider would help Hollman draft three letters to solicit funds from contacts in Grand Haven, Michigan for the cause.

As a sizable amount of circumstantial evidence grew that pointed to Hollman as the killer of Wiebke Geddes, it was revealed he had been heard making several disparaging remarks about the victim days before her death. This included him telling another "she was not fit to live."

Upon Hollman's arrest, investigators also began making a connection to the suspect and the murder of Carrie Lenz on November 28. Hollman had ignorantly revealed information to people he had encountered along his path about both crime scenes that only the actual murderer would know.

Chris Walters and John Bushman told authorities Hollman had spoke to them about an event "up north" that involved legal action.

Walters explained Hollman had said "a lawsuit up north took all my money, $40," and that he was broke when he stayed with them.

"Hollman said he was out of money," John Bushman recalled, when he stayed at his residence. "He said he spend it on a lawsuit in Chicago."

The event Hollman alluded to was his arrest in Waukegan, Illinois, when he was discovered hiding under a woman's bed inside of her home. Hollman had been sentenced to time in the jail after being convicted with breaking and entering.

After reviewing materials presented against the accused the Grand Jury brought in an indictment for murder against Frederick Hollman. He was returned to the Ford County jailhouse to be held for trial for the April 1897 term of court.

Behind the scenes, investigators were concerned over the lack of physical evidence in both the Geddes and Lenz murders. Two key items directly connecting Hollman to the murder victims were nowhere to be found.

It was reported that authorities believed a gold watch belonging to Carrie Lenz and a "Sollingen" shaving razor belonging to Fred Geddes still remained hidden somewhere at the Stuhmer farm.

Adding to the mystery was information from members of the Stuhmer family, who told authorities that Hollman had "gone away for a short time" on Sunday morning, December 6. Hollman was arrested that evening.

When questioned, Hollman said he had put on his coat that morning because there was a light rain and headed to the residence of August Misch. Hollman said he wished to pay the man a visit, but due to a light rain explained he "went about 60 rods (320 yards), turned around, then came back" to the Stuhmer farmhouse.

Authorities did not buy the "visit" story.

They had witness information that the missing items had been in Hollman's coat pocket and surmised he had discarded or "hidden the incriminating articles" at this time.

"Recognizing its importance as evidence, a posse was made up in this city on Monday, December 7, and bloodhounds were procured from Decatur," one newspaper reported.

Hollman's shoes were retained to give the dogs a scent and the posse was led straight to a haystack 330 yards from the Stuhmer farmhouse.

This process was repeated, and the stacks were carefully searched. A barn was reported searched, but the Lenz gold wrist watch and Geddes shaving razor were not found.

"Apparently if he had hidden anything there he (Hollman) had removed it to a more secure place," a newspaper reported.

Kevin Collier

PART 4

Hollman in Custody

Word spread authorities that were confident they had the man who killed Wiebke Geddes locked up. They were nearly certain they also had the killer of Carrie Lenz. Frederick Hollman was also named as the primary suspect in the death of Grethe Seifkin near Melvin in June that year, as investigators took another look at what had been ruled a suicide.

But while authorities were certain they had the right man, they did not know the true identity of whom they had in custody.

They would have plenty of time to figure it out and build a case against the prisoner, however, since Hollman would remain under lock and key until a trial in April 1897.

Authorities invited witnesses to the jailhouse where they could make positive identifications of Hollman. A photo was taken of the prisoner shortly after his incarceration which investigators used to provide further identification as they followed leads.

But who was this prisoner?

Everyone was calling him Fred, but Fred who?

Newspaper reporters covering the prisoner used a variety of names from Hoeltman to Hellman, but most reporters used the name Fred Hartman. It was the name Hollman had given when he was arrested on December 6 and the name written into the court document.

Hollman's arrest made the newspapers in and around Ford County, Illinois as it happened. Some newspapers in Wisconsin in and near Milwaukee jumped on the story within days. However, it took nearly three months before the Grand Haven Tribune of Michigan first published an article concerning Hollman's plight.

In March 1897 when news of his arrest and the charges reached his former hometown of Grand Haven, Michigan, it seemingly went unnoticed. Virtually no one recalled the man, and those who did vaguely remembered a "William Holman," the name he used when a resident.

After Constable Ira Gilmore locked up Hollman in the Ford County jail, on Sunday December 6, Benjamin Franklin Mason, the Sheriff of Ford County took charge of the prisoner.

Mason met Hollman for the first time the next day on December 7 at his examination before Justice of the Peace Jacob W. Preston.

Born in 1833, Sheriff Mason had been elected and served the county in the capacity of sheriff twice. His first term ran from 1886 to 1890. The second had begun in 1894. Mason had also served as a soldier in the Union Army throughout the Civil War.

The part of the jailhouse was a home for the Sheriff and his family, part was a temporary prison for criminals awaiting trial.

When it came to the jail, it was said Mason kept the cells neat and virtually spotless. He was kind to prisoners and often was sensitive to their needs.

When it came to the house part, Mason lived at the building with his wife of 45 years, Eliza, and a 33-year-old daughter named Nora. Mason was described as a "small man" in stature but "full of nerve." He acted like a man of age 40, not 63, which he was.

Sheriff Mason's relationship with Frederick Hollman would prove to be one of high emotion and spiritual challenge.

In his first act of kindness, Mason provided Hollman with a German language Bible. At the time, Hollman reportedly cursed and refused to read it. He refused to see any clergymen, as well.

The other prisoners at the jail were said to be sympathetic to Hollman and supported his claims of innocence.

Soon after Hollman's incarceration, physicians examined him and could not make a determination if he showed any symptoms of insanity.

Hollman was interrogated aggressively by investigators.

He repeatedly avoided pinpointing his exact whereabouts at the time of the Geddes and Lenz murders and it was reported he became "excited and contradicts himself" when questioned about it.

Sheriff Mason, along with Deputy Vinton Flora, began to follow new leads in hopes of finding items reportedly stolen from the Lenz and Geddes homes that remained missing.

Apparently the "chicken buyer" dialog Hollman had used in the company of others was not just a ruse to gain access into the homes of victims.

The venture was traced to the ACME Produce House in Bloomington, where Hollman had intended to sell the chickens. According to Hollman, the buyer was paying 12 cents a pound, nearly three times market value. The company then dressed the birds for market and shipped them from Saybrook (just south of Anchor) by rail to Joliet.

From this lead, information surfaced on a possible address for Frederick Hollman at 118 East Front Street in Bloomington. Some reports indicated the address was discovered on a receipt at the ACME produce house.

When Sheriff Mason and his men called on the address, it turned out to be the residence of "Mrs. Robert Campbell."

Eliza C. Campbell, a 67-year-old widow, was "a woman who did not rank high in public estimation," one newspaper reported. She not only knew Hollman, but appeared to be a friend. Mason and his men found a photograph displayed in her home she had taken of herself posing with Hollman.

Authorities confiscated the picture.

While questioning Campbell, Mason learned Hollman had recently given the woman a "silver" or "nickel" ladies wrist watch. Newspapers reported the watch matched the description of the one owned by Carrie Lenz.

However, there is no report of authorities seizing a watch from the Campbell residence, but it is possible, as Campbell would later identify the watch given to her by Hollman.

It had been reported a similar watch was found by Constable Ira Gilmore in Hollman's possession at the time of his arrest. Whether it was the same watch he had given Campbell and had somehow taken it back, is unknown.

What is clear is a "silver" or "nickel" ladies wrist watch authorities believed had belonged to Carrie Lenz would be placed into evidence by the prosecutor.

Sheriff Mason and his party departed the Campbell home confident the woman knew nothing about any crimes Hollman may have committed.

When confronted with information a watch had been retrieved, Hollman claimed he had purchased the silver watch given to Eliza Campbell at 217 Clark Street in Chicago. Hollman was furious newspapers were reporting a "silver" or "nickel" watch was found among his belongings when he was arrested by Constable Gilmore.

Hollman said that report "was a mistake," and Gilmore had not found any such watch in his possession.

But Gilmore stood by his assertion that he had taken the watch from Hollman when he arrested him.

The other missing watch owned by Carrie Lenz had not turned up. Thus, Hollman was questioned about "the gold watch" he had displayed and tried to sell after her murder.

Hollman explained that it was "a man's gold watch," not woman's, and he had acquired this one while in Chicago, too.

When confronted concerning the whereabouts of this watch, Hollman responded, "I sold the man's gold watch in Bloomington."

Mason and his team approached several pawnbrokers in Bloomington but a receipt of sale bearing Hollman's name for a gold watch never surfaced.

While in jail, Hollman had assembled a "whole package" of newspaper clippings which he kept in his pocket all reporting on the brutal murders of at least 20 other women. He produced the individually folded articles from his collection in comparison to the case being brought against him with a sense of his vindication.

"Here is one like my case," Hollman said, pulling out one of the articles and handing it to a jailhouse reporter. The clipping reported the robbery and murder of 90-year-old Caroline Bengle of Secor, Illinois. Hollman reportedly gloated as he pointed out details of the killing and errors in the investigation.

As newspapers reported details of the evidence mounting against Hollman, an angry mob of residents formed in nearby Drummer Township. A plan involved organizing with other groups from Melvin and Danforth and for a combined force to launch an attack on the jailhouse with intentions to lynch the accused.

On December 16, 1896, the mob acted out their intensions and appeared outside of the Paxton jailhouse shouting and holding incendiary placards. However, Hollman was no longer being held there.

Sheriff Mason got wind of the plot in advance and had already moved the prisoner. Initially, Hollman was moved to the Urbana jail in neighboring Champaign County under the authority of Sheriff Daniel Cannon.

The plot was likely thwarted when an informant told 61-year-old Charles C. Houdyshell, a city marshall who lived in Drummer Township, about the plan. Houdyshell, well-liked and respected, worked with Sheriff Mason.

A few days after Hollman was moved, chatter surfaced in Urbana that an angry mob was planning to attack the jail there with to bust Hollman out and lynch him.

Without incident, Hollman was secretly moved to the smaller, yet more secure jailhouse in Danville, Vermilion County, under the authority of Sheriff James Sloan.

The formation of angry mobs with intent to break prisoners out of jail for lynching was not an unusual occurrence at the time.

Conservative Illinois citizens in overwhelming numbers were frequently taking the law into their own hands due to Governor John Altgeld's disturbing record of releasing murderers from prisons.

In a two year period from 1893 to 1895, Altgeld had released 22 murderers from Illinois penitentiaries.

In 1893, two attempts by mobs to break killers Harvey Pate and Frank Stires out of the Danville jail with the intension of lynching them had been disrupted.

On May 24, 1895, two prisoners, John Halls, Jr. and William Royce, were abducted from the Danville jail by an angry mob and lynched.

"Yes, we know the jury will convict them (Halls and Royce) and give them a severe sentence, but Governor Altgeld will pardon them out," the Paterson Daily Press reported.

Two years earlier, Altgeld pardoned three men sentenced to 20 years in prison who committed crimes in Champaign County.

Theodore Roosevelt, before an audience of 13,000 cheering partisans in Chicago, said Altgeld was "one who would connive at wholesale murder," who "condones and encourages the most infamous of murders."

Many newspapers were calling Governor Altgeld "a killer's best friend."

If townsfolk of Ford County believed their Governor was "a killer's best friend," they might have imagined Hollman would receive even more favor as he, like Altgeld, was born German.

Sheriff Mason's decision to move Hollman to the jail in Urbana and especially Danville, was due to their experience with handling lynch mobs, and the increased security at both locations as a result of it.

The first interview with Frederick Hollman that appeared in print was on the final day of 1896. A reporter was granted an interview with the prisoner, which was published in the December 31 edition of the Paxton Record.

It is unknown if the interview took place before Hollman was moved from the Ford County jail, or after, at the Urbana or Danville jailhouses.

For two hours, speaking in broken English, Hollman outlined his whereabouts from October 1 to his moments before his arrest on December 6.

Much of his published statement is factually incorrect, either due to interpretation, or more likely, deception.

In the interview, Hollman stated his father, named Julius, owned 80 acres of farmland in Ripon, Wisconsin. It was added Julius was in possession of $300 owed to him.

However, Julius was Frederick's brother. His father, Charles, was deceased. There was no evidence the sibling owned 80 acres of farmland in Ripon. But Hollman would maintain in months ahead that his brother Julius owed him $300.

"I know that he (Julius) will assist me," Hollman said. "Those Germans at Paxton want to hang me, but they've got the wrong man. They also said I killed Mrs. Seifkin, who was murdered last spring," he continued.

In the interview, Hollman focused on the date of December 1, one day prior to the death of Wiebke Geddes, and explained his whereabouts. But while his encounters with others seemed to correspond with those police interviewed, the dates were all wrong.

Hollman said he was at the home of Harry Stevenson on December 1 and departed there to the home of Chris and Katie Walters, where he stayed for the night.

According to the Walters, Hollman had stayed at their residence on November 30.

Hollman claimed he awoke the day of Wiebke Geddes' murder and departed the Walters' home about 7:30 the morning of December 2 then stopped at the Stuhmer farmhouse where he was hired to pick corn.

"I never saw Mrs. Geddes," Hollman said.

But, according to Margaret Voss, neighbor and friend of Wiebke Geddes, she recalled encountering Hollman inside the Geddes residence during a routine visit days prior to the murder. Wiebke Geddes invited Voss in and requested she stay until Hollman departed. She then told Voss Hollman had frightened her, making "vile" proposals.

By January 1897, things had settled down a bit and Hollman was escorted from the jailhouse in Danville back to Paxton and placed under tighter security.

Sheriff Mason appointed Marshall Charles C. Houdyshell to serve as Hollman's personal jailhouse guard.

Houdyshell, a civil war veteran, born on August 4, 1835, lived alone with his wife Rebecca in Gibson City. Their only child, Warren, had died in 1878.

News surfaced that authorities in Wisconsin were seeking information on a man they considered a suspect in the murder of Anna Catherine Mohr in the town of Somers on September 21, 1896.

Wisconsin Attorney General Albert Ellsworth Buckmaster established communication with Sheriff Mason attempting to gain a positive identification of their suspect as being the prisoner lodged at Paxton. Mason mailed a copy of the photograph taken at the Ford County jailhouse of Hollman in early December to Buckmaster's office.

On January 11, 1897, Buckmaster confirmed the identity of the man wanted in murder of Anna Catherine Mohr was in fact Frederick Hollman. The suspect had been using the name of Fred Lang in the vicinity of Somers, Wisconsin at the time.

Anna Catherine Mohr's son, Andrew Mohr, also identified Hollman from the photograph circulated by Wisconsin authorities as "being in the neighborhood" at the time of his mother's death.

Mohr said Hollman had been at their residence the end of August or first week of September 1896 seeking work.

Andrew Mohr also confirmed the suspect was "using the name Fred Lang."

Neighbors of the Mohrs also identified the suspect for authorities from his photo and some recalled Hollman had asked if Mrs. Mohr and her son "lived alone."

The Grand Haven Tribune office reported it received a photo of Frederick Hollman on March 19, 1897 from Sheriff Mason for identification purposes during the pre-trial investigation.

The Tribune did not publish it, but used it to identify the subject when writing local articles of people who knew Hollman when he had lived in the city a decade or more earlier.

Soon Hollman became the chief suspect in the attempted murder of as many as eight other women, besides the rarely reported "six" he was suspected of killing, all of German descent.

A theory behind the gruesome murders arose claiming it stemmed from Frederick Hollman's hatred of his second wife, Augusta. A publication surmised Hollman's embitterment toward her had manifested into "a hatred of all women."

"He brooded over this until his paramount desire was to gratify some of his animal instincts and then kill women," the report said. "The theory is, that with this thought uppermost in his mind, he began a career of slaughter."

In early March 1897, Illinois State Attorney Abraham Lincoln Phillips announced to the press a single charge of murder would be leveled against Frederick Hollman. Phillips, who would prosecute the case, indicated the trial would commence in the April term of court in Paxton.

When news got out that Hollman was charged only with the murder of Wiebke Geddes, there was outrage in the community. He was not charged with, nor would be prosecuted for the death of Carrie Lenz, nor Grethe Seifkin.

The decision came from a grand jury which had convened. The jury determined which of the three deaths possessed the strongest evidence that would likely result in a successful prosecution.

While the murders of Grethe Seifkin and Carrie Lenz possessed strong evidence pointing to Hollman as the killer, it was determined these cases depended too heavily on circumstantial evidence.

Key physical evidence, such as the gold wrist watch, tying Hollman to the murder of Carrie Lenz was missing. The murder of Grethe Seifkin mainly involved witnesses that had seen and spoken to Hollman near the Seifkin farmhouse.

Evidence was strongest in the murder of Wiebke Geddes and the prosecution was confident this case would secure a first degree murder conviction. They reasoned it was better for Hollman to be hanged for one murder, than risk a "not guilty" verdict where he would walk.

The decision enraged Matthias Bauman, the father of Carrie Lenz.

Bauman had appeared before the grand jury to plead a case for a charge murder against Hollman for the death of his daughter. The jury denied his request.

Matthias Bauman was a well-known jeweler in the city of Gilman in Iroquois County, where his daughter had been murdered. He lived in nearby Danforth, about 4 miles north.

After the decision was announced to only prosecute Hollman for the death of Wiebke Geddes, Bauman petitioned the court that in the event Hollman was found not guilty (or given a light sentence) charges could be brought against him in the death of his daughter.

Bauman was convinced the evidence that Hollman had murdered his eldest daughter was overwhelming and did not want Hollman to escape justice.

Some residents in Danforth were near uprising over the decision not to charge Hollman with the murder Carrie Lenz.

"Lately there has been considerable talk in the vicinity of Danforth of a party organizing and going down from there to get Hollman," The Gibson City Courier reported.

The intent of the Danforth posse was to lynch Hollman.

Matthias Bauman was not involved in the organization of the movement, nor did he approve of it. Surprisingly, it was he who appealed to those hatching the plan to abandon the idea, which they did.

It was later learned that Bauman had been assured in private that Hollman would be brought to trial for the murder of his daughter if a conviction was not achieved in the Geddes case.

Reverend M. Toewe of St. John's German Lutheran Church in Grand Haven was one of three individuals who received a letter from Frederick Hollman's attorney Columbus Schneider on his behalf, with the intention to solicit funds for his defense.

The letter Toewe received stated that "a man was in jail" in Paxton, Illinois and "charged with murder. The letter read, "Fred Hollman, a former Grand Haven man is in serious danger of being executed in Illinois."

"Hollman wants his former church people to help him," the message continued. "$100 would assist him greatly in the fight for his life, which will soon come up." In closing, Schneider wrote, "If we do not get $100, so that we may gather all the information necessary, Hollman will be hanged, as there is strong circumstantial evidence."

Hollman had indicated Reverend Christopher Zimmerman was the pastor of the church when he was a member.

The letter, however, was delivered to the wrong church.

It was supposed to be addressed to St. Paul's German Evangelical Lutheran Church, not St. John's, the other Lutheran Church in the city.

Reverend Toewe of St. John's turned the letter over to Reverend Lars Hagen, current pastor of St. Paul's German Evangelical Lutheran Church, which was the church Hollman had once been a member.

Frederick Hollman's cousin, Charlie Hallman, also received a letter asking for $100.

Another letter with a $100 request was delivered to friend Wilburt Thieleman.

Thieleman was saloonkeeper at 8 Washington Street, next door to the Kirby House. He was also a wholesale representative for the Schlitz Brewing Company for 20 years at the location. Thieleman had also helped organize St. Paul's German Evangelical Lutheran Church.

Besides the three Grand Haven solicitations, Hollman had informed Schneider that his brother Julius Hallman, who lived in Ripon, Wisconsin, owed him $300.

However, attempts to reach Julius Hallman did not produce results. It appeared he had left the state and moved on.

When it came to raising money for Frederick Hollman's defense, there is no evidence St. Paul's German Evangelical Lutheran Church ever contributed a penny to it.

Neither did his cousin, Charlie Hallman, or friend Wilburt Thieleman.

Those who recalled Hollman remembered him for beating his first wife, Amelia, and Hollman had been mobbed by the German citizens in Grand Haven for abusing his second wife Augusta as well. Distain for Hollman was still present and locals were not inclined to help.

One anonymous source in Grand Haven, who knew Hollman well, said he always thought the accused would come to "some bad end" because he seemed to be "very brutal towards women."

"Instead of sending money to aid him, I'd rather send money to prosecute the fellow," the unidentified man told the Grand Haven Tribune.

"His lawyer (Columbus Schneider) tried to get financial help from this city, but it was not forthcoming, because of the fact that Hollman was altogether too well known," the Grand Haven Tribune reported.

"Too well known" for his brutal reputation.

Frederick Hollman sat in the Ford County jailhouse at Paxton over four months awaiting trial. During his incarceration he made many suspicious and revealing statements, much of this made its way into newspapers.

In January 1897, William Kelly, a 46-year-old petty thief, began serving time at the jailhouse. Kelly had stolen a turkey worth $1.46 and was convicted on a technicality of burglary and received a three month sentence.

At times Kelly was placed in the same cell with Frederick Hollman where the two engaged in many conversations.

Once Hollman told Kelly of "a dutch farmer (who) was doing life in (a) Wisconsin (prison)," and that he believed the man's name was "Hilgendorf or Higgendorf."

Hollman relayed to Kelly that the man convicted of that murder was "innocent" and that he and an accomplice had actually murdered the man's wife.

However, Kelly never shared this conversation with anyone at the time.

William Kelly considered himself "a close friend" of Hollman during their time in jail together and revealed Hollman's jail cell confession in a sworn statement on November 29, 1898, nearly a year and a half after it took place.

Kelly's trial took place just days before Hollman's trial began.

There were as many as six other men lodged at the jail awaiting trial between January and April that year. The included; brothers John and Harry Harris, Fred Hamer, Samuel Stange, Middleton Galbraith, and Charles Lyons. The charges against the prisoners ranged from public drunkenness to intent to commit murder.

It is possible Hollman could have had opportunities to speak with any of these men, too, regarding the crimes for which he was accused.

Newspapers or periodicals featuring information about the Frederick Hollman were routinely kept from his reach.

He did not like the press.

"They spread lies," Hollman once said.

However, Sheriff Benjamin Mason often brought the Hollman books and magazines to his cell. Hollman appreciated the lawman's kindness.

Hollman's personal collection of print stories had grown since displaying a pocketful of news clippings to a reporter and others shortly after his arrest.

The assortment, which he kept in his cell, included actual and fictional stories of violence and murders committed upon helpless women and girls.

The Chicago Tribune reported that the clippings were mainly torn from "sensational (tabloid) weekly" publications, much like pulp magazines, giving accounts of random murders and acts of cruelty.

"These articles he reads again and again and gloats over the details of the most revolting crimes, the most barbaric displays of cruelty, and malice inflicted upon women," the Chicago Tribune explained.

Charles C. Houdyshell, Hollman's jailhouse guard, observed that Hollman paid particular attention to the sensational details concerning the methods used in the murders, actual and fictitious. Apparently, Houdyshell was uncertain if allowing Hollman to possess such a collection was a good idea.

"Hollman confines his conversations to his escapades with women," Howdyshell told a reporter. "He says he has associated with women of the vilest class for years."

As details of his peculiar and suspicious behavior in jail began making the pages of local newspapers, some raised a concern if Hollman could get a fair trial in Ford County. A change of venue for the trial in a neighboring county was discussed, but was denied by the court.

The newspapers were putting items to print that made the prisoner appear to be a malicious, manipulating monster.

Word leaked to the press that Hollman attempted to get his attorney to assist in the destruction of evidence that would be used in his trial. Hollman told his Columbus Schneider he wanted him to bring to his cell the clothing he was wearing the morning Wiebke Geddes was murdered.

Hollman then could "cut the garments into small strips and dispose of them."

Schneider, obviously, denied the request and did not hand over the garments.

What the press failed to report was Columbus Schneider visited Hollman in his jail cell frequently, and not always in the capacity of an attorney, but in a spiritual sense.

The public read that Hollman had threatened to beat up any preacher that tried to enter his cell. According to the newspapers, the point of contention was the denial of administering communion. Lutheran ministers would not allow Hollman to take communion until he had confessed to the sin of murder. Hollman refused, claiming his innocence.

It would be revealed later that Columbus Schneider often prayed with Hollman and read scripture with him initially filling that void.

To what degree Hollman actually immersed himself in scripture while awaiting trial in unknown. One published report claimed Hollman did not begin reading the Bible provided to him by Sheriff Mason until after his sentencing at trial.

However, it was reported Hollman had in his possession his own Bible, one he had brought with him from Brandenburg, Germany, and that he turned to scripture frequently in moments of solitude.

Frederick Hollman had occasional visitors in jail while awaiting trial.

One was Andrew Mohr, son of Anna Catherine Mohr, the woman Hollman was suspected of murdering in Somers, Wisconsin on September 20, 1896.

Andrew Mohr paid a visit to the Ford County jail to meet with Hollman to urge him to confess to the murder of his mother. Hollman told Mohr that he would make no admission of guilt, but did provide an eerie observation only the killer would posses.

Hollman admitted to have been in the neighborhood where Anna Catherine Mohr was murdered and gave a brief description of the manner in which the woman was killed.

"She had been choked until nearly dead," Hollman said, as if he was recalling a newspaper article he had read. "Then a string was tied around her neck and tied to a door knob."

Andrew Mohr departed without receiving a confession, reason, or closure.

While awaiting trial, Hollman attempted to commit suicide "several times" according to one newspaper. Thus, he was kept under close watch and guard.

A pocket knife was found in the toe of his shoe and confiscated.

Hollman also asked his attorney Columbus Schneider for poison at one time, to be used if he should be sentenced to death.

There was one thing Hollman's visitors could agree on, that he was persistent in his claims of innocence. It was "a surprise' to all who talked to him, knowing the horrid details reported about "his victims" in the local newspapers.

But depending on which newspaper one read, reports often conflicted concerning Hollman's behavior. While he was no angel, at times he was presented as man possessing the attributes of discipline and virtue.

"He is polite to all who come near him," The Pantagraph reported. The Bloomington newspaper went on to say that Hollman had been a "model prisoner" and was "attentive to rules."

After months in jail, it was reported at times that Hollman was full of jokes and ready to play pranks on his attendants. He often invited them to sing hymns with him in his cell in a joyous fashion.

Then, a moment later, Hollman would be sobbing or fly into a rage.

He was able to change moods in a matter of minutes.

He was said to be "an enigma," by those closest to him.

Newspapers around the nation were picking up and republishing reports originating from Ford County about the accused.

"Fake" jailhouse interviews with Frederick Hollman were reported to be in circulation.

Hollman distrusted the press and claimed he never granted such "an exclusive" to any newspaper. There is evidence that he did.

While some quotes attributed to Hollman may have been "fake," an interview, or obtained exclusive question and answer arrangement, likely did not occur more than twice.

What usually happened was Sheriff Mason, on occasion, would allow a reporter to hang out near Hollman's cell. If lucky, the reporter would arrive when someone else was in the cell with Hollman and hear something they could write down. Sometimes the reporters acquired some amazing quotes, sometimes not.

Some reporters dared not to try to talk to the man, while some tried and were cursed at.

Where some newspapers got some of their information from remains uncertain. Like the Kansas City Journal, which reported that Hollman was "believed to have killed a number of women in Illinois, Indiana and Michigan."

There was no evidence Hollman was linked to any unsolved murders in Indiana and Michigan. However, there was evidence beginning to surface that implicated Hollman in a 1895 murder near Hanover, Pennsylvania.

Kevin Collier

PART 5

The Trial and Aftermath

Jury selection for the trail of Frederick Hollman took place on April 8 and 9, 1897. Fifty-nine men were examined before the panel was complete.

All of the men were from Gibson City and neighboring townships. They came from different walks of life and ranged in age from 35 to 56.

The men were:

Weaver White, a farmer, age 48, born in Ohio, resident of Paxton, where he lived with his wife Arrabella and their three children.

Augustus A. Moffett, a day laborer, age 48, born in Indiana, resident of Paxton, where he lived with his wife Mattie and their three children.

Arthur H. Dillon, musical instrument salesman, age 44, born in Illinois, resident of Paxton, where he lived with his wife Mary and child Stella.

Henry Lindgren, a farmer, age 38, born in Indiana, resident of Button Township, where he lived with Susan and their two children.

George Ewing McCracken, a grocer, age 35, born Indiana, resident of Paxton, where he lived with his wife Anna and three children.

William Taylor Morrison, a farmer, age 56, born in Ohio, resident of Paxton, where he lived with his wife Mary and five children.

David B. Graves, age 50, born in Pennsylvania, resident of Paxton, where he lived with his wife Mary and their daughter.

William Wallace Reser, farmer, age 53, born in Indiana, resident of Paxton, where he lived with his wife J. Emma. They had eight children.

John T. Stewart, a druggist, age 44, born in Illinois, resident of Paxton, where he lived with his wife Susan and two children.

Erastus McHenry, a farmer, age 36, born in Pennsylvania, resident of the town of Clarence, where he lived with his wife Laura Jane and two children.

John Hutchinson, a farmer, age 43, born in Ohio, resident of Button Township, where he lived with his wife Jennie and five children.

Owen Connell Beagle, a farmer, age 42, born in Illinois, resident of Button Township, where he lived with his wife Mary and children.

The honorable Judge Alfred Sample presided over the Hollman murder trial.

Born in Butler County, Ohio on November 27, 1846, Sample took residence in Illinois in 1857. He was elected Circuit Judge in June 1885 of the eleventh judicial circuit, which comprised the counties of McLean, Ford, Livingston, Kankakee and Iroquois.

Alfred Sample was a respected veteran of the Civil War. In November 1863, when sixteen years of age, he enlisted in Company G, 129th Illinois Volunteer Infantry, and went immediately into active service.

Sample participated in General Sherman's campaign in the march to Atlanta. In the battle of Resaca he was severely wounded in both arms and chest. Unfit for continued duty, Sample was honorably discharged on December 6, 1864.

Sample had also served as presidential elector for James Garfield in 1880, was Illinois State Attorney from 1872 until 1880, and city attorney from 1873 until 1877.

The Hollman murder trial would be one of last cases over which Judge Sample would preside.

Overwhelmed by the experience, he retired the two months later in June 1897.

Illinois State Attorney Abraham Lincoln Phillips was the lead prosecutor in the case. Columbus S. Schneider, assisted by Frank Fulton, would represent Hollman's defense.

Columbus S. Schneider went into the trial feeling confident. He told the Pantagraph that he "cared very little for the evidence" against his client, as "it was all circumstantial." However, Schneider's client would prove to be a courtroom nightmare.

The case against Frederick Hollman involved little physical evidence and had to rely on the testimony of many witnesses to piece together a circumstantial case that offered no other conclusion than Hollman was the murderer of Wiebke Geddes.

Prosecutor Abraham Phillips would have to construct a timeline of events from murder of Carrie Lenz, without making her the topic of discussion, to the day of Hollman's arrest, 4 days after the murder of Wiebke Geddes. Phillips would have to convince the jury that Hollman's injuries were the result of a struggle with the deceased and that they did not occur, or were seen by anyone, until after she was killed.

Phillips would have to walk a careful line during the trial introducing information as Hollman was only on trial for the death of Wiebke Geddes. He could bring it to the jury's awareness in regards to establishing Hollman's said whereabouts, but the defendant was not on trial for any other death. Phillips could try to trap Hollman in lies and thus put the defendant's credibility in question.

The biggest concern for Phillips was Fred Geddes' stolen shaving razor, which was said by many to be in Hollman's possession, but was never found. Phillips would have to depend on eyewitnesses accounts of seeing that item on the defendant to place it in his hands.

To his client's advantage, defense attorney Columbus Schneider knew that when the razor appeared inside the Stuhmer farmhouse, it was first seen on the kitchen floor. From there it became a topic of discussion within the family, and

Louise Stuhmer secretly took it from Hollman to show others in an attempt to positively identify it as the one owned by Fred Geddes.

The problem was that children of the Stuhmer family had been playing in the coats hung in the kitchen and the garments had fallen to the floor. Louise Stuhmer assumed the razor had fallen out of Hollman's coat pocket, so she put it back there. She could not say for certain it had come from Hollman's pocket.

Adding to the confusion, another man who was employed at the farm wore a similar coat. His coat had been hung alongside Hollman's in the kitchen. He quit work shortly after hiring on, and right after Louise Stuhmer found the razor. He was not heard from again nor could anyone recall his name. This created a "mystery man" who Schneider could exploit in the jury's mind as being the man who was the "chicken buyer" and the true killer.

The watches missing from the Lenz home could only be presented as stolen items that Hollman had tried to dispose. Carrie Lenz's gold watch never surfaced. It is uncertain if Wiebke Geddes' pocketbook was ever clearly identified as Prosecutor Phillips virtually sidelined it. Apparently, a gold ring owned by Mrs. Geddes her husband reported stolen was never shown to anyone, never surfaced, and was only briefly touched upon.

Frederick Hollman's appearance during the proceedings described the accused as disheveled and unshaven, which would not aid his defense. His erratic behavior would also keep his attorney on edge and feeling uneasy.

The murder trial in Ford County was a shocking affair that drew a sizable crowd at the courtroom.

It was reported during the proceedings that upwards of a hundred or more onlookers gained entrance to the courtroom with far more standing outside discussing the event.

Present for the duration of the trial was Albert A. Hofmann, the Official Court Reporter.

Hofmann began reporting in the Ford county circuit court and the Bloomington court in 1885 and in 1887 when a law appointing Official Reporters went into effect.

Hofmann had reported many cases in the counties of McLean, De Witt, Tazewell and Livingston. This would be his biggest case as official journalist. Much of the news printed in local newspapers was issued by Hofmann in the form of courtroom press releases. He also interpreted for German witnesses during the trial as he had done previously in other cases.

Many newspaper reporters in surrounding Illinois counties and from Chicago and Wisconsin placed correspondents at the courthouse to cover the proceedings. But many relied on Albert Hofmann's press releases as crowds packed the courtroom at times leaving members of the press standing in the halls or outdoors.

Stories from some of these newspapers were presented as summaries or reprinted in full by the Grand Haven Tribune in Hollman's former hometown. The Tribune supplemented the articles adding local response, but Hollman's cousin Charlie Hallman declined requests to be interviewed and never spoke with the newspaper.

Memories of Frederick Hollman were still fresh in the minds of Grand Haven residents and those despised him.

"The man lived here some years ago," the Tribune reported, "and bore an unsavory reputation because of the brutality to his wife."

Opening statements at trial were presented by attorneys Phillips and Schneider in the early evening of April 9. Reportedly, each side spoke for two hours.

The story of the crime was presented to the jury as follows:

On the morning of December 2, 1896, the wife of Fred Geddes, who lived about nine miles northwest of Gibson, was found dead in her home. Her body was shockingly bruised, and was suspended by a rope fastened around the neck attached to a door knob.

Her husband, who had gone to work before daylight, was immediately summoned from the field, and broke down and cried at the terrible sight. The coroner's inquest developed nothing material as to the perpetrator of the deed, except that the little daughter, who was in the room when the murder was committed, had said that her "father had done it."

On this evidence, and from the fact that he was the last known person to leave the house that morning, Fred Geddes was bound over to the Grand Jury, and charged with the murder. The Grand Jury found the evidence insufficient to hold him, and he was dismissed on December 5.

Suspicion by this time began to point to a stranger named Hoellmann, of Hartman, who had spoken of buying chickens in the neighborhood about the time of the murder. He was found at the Stuhmer farm near the Geddes place, and was arrested.

The preliminary hearing brought out some strong evidence against the suspect, and he was bound over to the Grand Jury, which promptly returned an indictment charging him with the murder. Other murders similar to this one were also attributed to Hollman, and if there was anything in the rumors and reports that have gone around concerning his arrest, he was a veritable "Jack the Ripper."

Prosecuting Attorney displayed the only known photo of Wiebke Geddes to the jury. The picture, taken in Germany, was said to present "an intelligent and winning face." Phillips also added that the physician who examined Wiebke Geddes after her death testified that her physical perfections made her appearance to be "one of the finest women I have ever seen."

A missing piece of evidence spoken about at length during the trial was Fred Geddes' "Sollingen" razor, which remained missing. Placing the razor in Hollman's hands rested entirely on eyewitness accounts.

After the opening arguments court was dismissed until Saturday morning.

Kevin Collier

Testimony began Saturday morning, April 10. Owing to the fact that several of the witnesses spoke only German, Professor Rudolph H. H. Blome, of the Rice Collegiate Institute of Paxton, was employed to assist as an interpreter.

Testimony by Fred Geddes and Michael Voss presented that day had to be taken through an interpreter.

Fred Spaulding, age 23, a civil engineer, was called to prove the authenticity of plats and plans, the ascertation of the position of the land by design, diagram, maps or charts in evidence to be used in connection with the murder of Wiebke Geddes.

Fred Geddes Testifies

Fred Geddes, husband of the murdered woman, testified that on the morning of December 2, 1896, he arose about 4:30, dressed himself, blew out the lamplight, and went to the farm of John Stroh where he was at work shucking corn.

Geddes got out Stroh's team of horses and fed them, ate his breakfast, then went to the field.

At about 11 o'clock, a boy came into the field and told Geddes his wife was sick. Geddes asked if it was serious and the boy told him "no," so he husked out the rows he was at work upon, and then went home.

Arriving at his tenant residence on the farm, Geddes found his wife dead lying across a door sill, between the living and sleeping rooms. Geddes said he did not notice a spading fork, which had been standing upright against a wall, in the room. A pocketbook, which had contained five dollars in German bills and coins and his wife's gold ring, with her name engraved inside, were missing.

Another purse lay open on the table.

It is possible the ring had been misplaced, and was found in the home later, as the item neither fails to appear in further testimony nor mentioned as an exhibit in evidence.

Geddes mentioned that these items routinely had been kept in the cupboard, together with a shaving razor he had bought in the old country. The word "Sollingen" was on the blade, and "Kline" on the case.

Geddes was shown a purse in evidence, which was in the Hollman's possession at the time he was arrested. Geddes identified it as belonging to his wife.

Geddes was presented the cord found around the neck of his wife and on the door knob. He stated that nothing resembling its type was at their residence.

It was compared to the cord type from the Lenz murder scene.

"This cord or string is the same I found attached to the to the catch of the door," Geddes responded.

Fred Geddes testified he had married Wiebke in Germany seven years ago, and they had lived in this country two years. He told the court they had one child, Elizabeth, and the girl was 6 years old and had always been an invalid.

Fred Geddes relayed he had always lived happily with his wife and they "never shared a cross word."

Geddes was put through an extensive cross-examination on the witness stand by Hollman's attorney, Columbus Schneider.

Schneider brought up the fact that Geddes' own daughter had told neighbor Johanna Voss, 23-year-old daughter of Michael and Margaret, "and others" that "my bad papa done it," implicating her father.

Schneider aggressively attempted to pin the murder of Wiebke Geddes on her husband, a futile effort considering a grand jury had ruled Fred Geddes was not involved.

Schneider painted the Geddes as a quarrelsome couple and pointed out to the jury Fred Geddes did not act alarmed when John Stroh's son met him in the corn field to inform him his wife was ill.

Geddes explained to the jury his wife was subject routinely to severe headaches and that accounted for the reason for his lack of response to the message that she "was sick."

Fred Geddes did not own the spading folk that was used in part to kill his wife, and Schneider pressed him on how it came into his possession and why it had been hidden beneath the bed.

Geddes claimed he knew nothing about the spading fork being left under the bed of his home and explained, "It had been borrowed from Michael Voss to dig potatoes."

Geddes explained he searched his home the day of the murder, which is when he discovered his wife's purse and ring were missing. He admitted it was not until after he had been released from jail that his noticed his Sollingen razor was missing.

Geddes also admitted he had "searched the barn and surroundings" on the day of his wife's murder "to see if any tramps had been there," but found nothing.

Michael and Margaret Voss Testify

Michael Voss took the witness stand and testified he lived across the road from the Geddes home.

He recalled on the wintery morning of December 2 he was fixing a gate and became cold, so he went into Geddes's house around 8:30-9:00 to warm up. He did not knock, but walked right in.

When Voss opened the door he saw Wiebke Geddes lying on the floor between the living room and bedroom. He took hold of her arm and said she was "stark and cold."

Voss testified he saw Geddes' daughter, Elizabeth, sitting on the bed crying "Mamma, mamma." Voss tried to calm her and told her not to cry and that he would send for Auntie Voss (his wife Margaret) to come and get her.

Voss noted he did not stay inside the residence very long.

Voss ran across the road and summoned his wife and two daughters and sent his youngest daughter Mary to the Stroh's farm to inform him what had happened.

John Stroh Sr. and his wife rushed to the Geddes residence and looked about carefully.

A "string" was hanging on the door latch, and a small piece like it lay on the floor.

The dead woman was covered with wounds and black and blue spots.

On cross-examination, Columbus Schneider attempted to put into question the time Michael Voss actually discovered the scene.

Voss said he could not recall the exact time when he first entered the Geddes house but testified it could have been later, between 9:00 or 9:30 that morning.

When questioned why he had tampered with the victim's body, as it was a crime scene, Voss explained he only lifted the arm of the dead woman to determine whether she "was dead."

On redirect, Prosecutor Abraham Phillips asked the witness to better explain his family's relationship with the victim and her family, and whether he was aware of any friction in the Fred Geddes marriage.

Voss said his family and the Geddes were neighbors and "had always been good friends."

He added he never knew Fred and Wiebke Geddes to have any conflicts as husband and wife.

Voss also said he had observed "finger marks" on Elizabeth Geddes' neck, which appeared to be "very plain" (or defined) the next morning.

Margaret Voss took the witness stand and testified Frederick Hollman presented himself at the Geddes home a week before the murder claiming he was buying chickens and "paying eight cents a pound."

Margaret Voss testified she was a guest at the Geddes home at the moment of one of Hollman's visits there. She said Hollman had inquired about "the habits of Mr. Fred Geddes" concerning his morning routine.

According to Margaret Voss, Wiebke Geddes told Frederick Hollman her husband worked for John Stroh and "got up at 4 in the morning to feed the horses." She added Wiebke Geddes also told Hollman, "he receives his breakfast there before going to work on the farm."

Geddes' Employer John Stroh Sr. Testifies

John Stroh Sr. took the witness stand and testified that he lived in the main farmhouse on his property "one-fourth mile" from the Geddes' residence. He stated he rented that residence to the family.

Stroh identified the Ashley schoolhouse from graphic, and said it was located three miles from his place. He noted it was a place where Hollman "said he had stayed" two nights preceding the murder.

According to Stroh, Fred Geddes arrived at his house about 4:30 the morning of December 2, 1896.

After feeding the horses and taking breakfast in the farmhouse, Geddes went out to husk corn.

Stroh testified that Michael Voss' daughter, Mary Voss, came over and informed him that Mrs. Geddes was dead. He thought she was mistaken so sent his son out, John Stroh, Jr., to give word to Fred Geddes that his wife "was sick." He noted he did not want the man to receive news of his wife's death while he was in the field.

John Stroh, Sr. explained he then went to the Geddes residence to have a look.

He described the scene at Geddes' house, including the wounds on the victim, much in the same manner as Michael Voss had earlier.

Stroh said he sent a message by messenger to Gibson City for the coroner.

Stroh recalled when he went into the house Elizabeth Geddes said to him, "Papa came back and jumped onto mamma."

Stroh added the little girl said her mother responded, "Fred, Fred, is that you?" That had been all her mother had said, the daughter claimed. "Papa did not say anything," Elizabeth told Stroh.

Stroh relayed he found binding twine on the door latch.

"The body was black and blue all over," he said.

Upon examination, he noticed there was a depression in the back of Wiebke Geddes' head.

Stroh said he confronted Fred Geddes thinking him to be the killer and urged a confession.

"I said, come on," Stroh recalled, as he escorted Geddes to see the crime scene. "Tell me what is true. You got into a little racket or fight last night with your wife."

Stroh said Fred Geddes had laughed off information that his wife was dead until he arrived at the home and saw it was true.

Concerning the state of the Geddes marriage, Stroh said "Geddes and his wife were devoted to each other...The child (Elizabeth, a cripple) was sick a great deal and Geddes frequently spent all of their money earned for doctor services."

Stroh added Wiebke Geddes also earned a living to help provide for the family finances.

Cross-examination was postponed.

Doctor Frank O. Cutler Testifies

Doctor Frank O. Culter, age 36, of Gibson City, took the witness stand and testified that he made an examination of Wiebke Geddes' body the day of her funeral.

Culter explained it "was not a regular post mortem examination."

Culter explained Wiebke Geddes' right leg was broken between the knee and ankle and a wound was found on her left leg. There was a blue streak nine inches long across the bowels and another under the jaw that extending across the left side of her face to the ear. He thought her jaw had been broken.

The wounds on the bowels and jaw exactly fitted the spade fork tines.

The doctor examined a depression in her skull and observed discolorations all over her body. The depression in her skull was about the size of a silver quarter and was exactly fitted by the spading fork handle. He told the jury the wound in Wiebke's head would be fatal.

Culter explained he could not tell whether or not the woman had been sexually assaulted.

Hollman became disturbed at the mere mention of sexual assault and prompted his defense attorney challenge it.

The doctor described Wiebke Geddes as "well developed" and "strikingly handsome. She was apparently "above average" in intelligence.

The doctor testified that "a body will become rigid from thirty minutes to six hours after death," but he had known of one case where twenty-four hours first elapsed before rigor mortus set in.

During cross-examination, Columbus Schneider pressed Culter whether or not he "knew for a fact" the woman had been "violated" (or sexually assaulted).

"I do not think the woman had been violated," Cutler responded, "but it is possible."

When questioned concerning how long Mrs. Geddes had been dead before discovered, Culter said temperature had nothing to do with rigor mortis.

He added that he did not know when the woman was killed and explained a bruise turns black at varying periods of time after a blow is inflicted—it may be two hours or much longer.

Truman D. Spaulding Testifies

Truman D. Spaulding, age 58, foreman of the coroner's jury, took the witness stand and told the jury of the holding of the inquest into the murder of Wiebke Geddes.

He said young Elizabeth Geddes' testimony was "very unsatisfactory," as she could not speak English and cried continually.

Spaulding noted that he had assisted Doctor Frank Culter in an external examination of Mrs. Geddes' body.

On cross-examination by Columbus Schneider, Spaulding was asked about Elizabeth Geddes having pointed to her own father as the killer.

Spaulding said that Elizabeth Geddes had indeed declared at the inquest that her "father had killed her mother," and had repeated it. It was at that time Spaulding explained the jury recommended that Fred Geddes be held for the murder without bail.

"That was an honest opinion at the time," Spaulding said.

He admitted he felt some doubt as to the child's statement, thus went back to the Voss home the next day and questioned the child again "through an interpreter."

The proceedings for Saturday ended at that moment. There was no court on Sunday. Proceedings resumed on Monday, April 12.

Testimony at trial resumed on the morning of Monday, April 12. Many witnesses were called to the stand on that very busy day.

Charles C. Houdyshell Testifies

Deputy Sheriff Charles C. Houdyshell took the witness stand and testified in regard to the coroner's inquest, and the marks on the Wiebke Geddes' body.

Houdyshell said he arrived at the murder scene and said John Stroh Sr. and Henry Hendricks had urged him to summon a doctor to make an examination before allowing an undertaker to remove the body.

Houdyshell acknowledged he was the one who summoned Doctor Frank Culter and was present during the examination of the body.

His testimony corroborated the doctor's in regard to the condition of the body.

Houdyshell explained that he had issued subpoenas to witnesses for the Grand Jury, but was not part of the inquest.

Houdyshell recalled Doctor Cutler placing the spading fork on the wound on the back of Wiebke Geddes' head.

"It made a circle, like the tine (the prong or sharp point) of a fork," Houdyshell said.

He also relayed a chain of events concerning who arrived at the murder scene during the examination and how they had been contacted.

Coroner William A. Hutchison Testifies

Ford County coroner William A. Hutchison took the witness stand and testified he saw no mark on the back of

Kevin Collier

Wiebke Geddes head, and found no particular wound that was determined to have caused her death.

This contradicted the testimony of Charles Houdyshell and Doctor Frank Cutler.

Hutchison admitted he was "no skilled physician," but was in the room when Cutler examined the body further in his coroner's office.

Hutchison identified the piece of cord presented as an exhibit as being the one he found around Wiebke Geddes' neck and that he had handed the twine over to Sheriff Benjamin Mason.

He also identified the pair of shears found with Elizabeth Geddes, which she had used in an attempt to cut her mother down from the door.

John Stroh Jr., Joe Hanson, and Eliza C. Campbell Testify Briefly

John Stroh, Jr., the son of the owner of the Stroh farm, took the witness stand and testified as to the appearance of Wiebke Geddes on the day of the murder.

Stroh said that when he informed Fred Geddes that his wife had been murdered, Geddes laughed and laughed again.

He added that when they arrived at the house and Fred Geddes saw the dead body of his wife, he broke down and cried.

Joe Hanson from the village of Elliott testified took the witness stand next. He was the brother of Claus Hanson.

Hanson said that he knew the Geddes family well, and that the couple lived together happily. He said Wiebke Geddes thought she "couldn't get a better husband."

Hanson said he had seen the shaving razor described in testimony and knew it to be owned by Fred Geddes. He stated he had shaved with it once when Fred Geddes came over from Germany two years ago.

On cross-examination, Columbus Schneider questioned Hanson as to the financial burden the Geddes' daughter,

Elizabeth, posed to the relationship between the husband and wife.

"Their child, Lizzie, is six years old. She has a bad back and is wearing a corset now that cost $25." Hanson added.

He explained while the cost was a burden, Fred and Wiebke Geddes had a happy marriage.

Hanson described the garments Hollman wore at the time of the murder in the same way others would testify at the trial. "He wore a Scotch cap and a gray overcoat."

Eliza C. Campbell, a 67-year-old widow residing in Bloomington, took the witness stand and identified Frederick Hollman as the man she had her photograph taken with that authorities found on display in her home.

Campbell said Hollman had been kind and friendly to her. It is unknown if defense attorney Columbus Schneider questioned Campbell concerning her "reputation" around Bloomington. It was rumored Campbell was a woman of questionable ethics.

Campbell testified that Hollman had given her a ladies wrist watch, and identified the item presented in evidence. Prosecutor Phillips stated authorities believed it was stolen and belonged to Carrie Lenz, who was murdered on November 26, 1896.

James Gray Testifies

James Gray, who lived four miles southwest of Gibson City, took the witness stand and testified to meeting a man answering the description of Frederick Hollman on the highway near his home before Wiebke Geddes was murdered.

Gray recalled it was "evening and intolerably dark at the time." Gray estimated he was 20-30 feet from Hollman during their encounter and paid particular notice of him because "there had been chicken thieves reported in the vicinity."

Gray said the Hollman had been at the home of Michael Voss, across the road from the Geddes residence, as he and Margaret Voss had spoken about it.

According to Gray, Hollman told the same story wherever he went.

"He was buying chickens for shipment," Gray recalled.

Chris Stroh and John Brandt Testify

Andrea Christian Stroh, known as Chris, who was the brother of John Stroh Sr., landowner of the farm where Wiebke Geddes was murdered, took the witness stand but offered little.

Stroh testified he saw Hollman on Tuesday, December 1, the day before the murder, shelling corn. Stroh noted he resided one-half mile north of his cousin Claus Stroh, who owned a farm on southwest corner of Sullivant Township.

John Brandt of Sullivant Township took the witness stand and said he spoke with Frederick Hollman on Monday, November 30.

This encounter occurred after the murder of Carrie Lenz but before the murder of Wiebke Geddes.

The location where he met Hollman was two and a half miles northwest of the Geddes residence. Brandt said Hollman told him he "had to leave Wisconsin on account of a girl scrape."

Brandt said Hollman stated that he and his brothers owned two 80 acres of farmland in Wisconsin, nearly all of it being tile drained. Brandt recalled Hollman was posing as a chicken buyer.

"He said he wanted to get the chickens Thanksgiving day," Brandt said.

Chris and Katie Walters Testify

Chris Walters, who resided with his wife Katie five miles north-east of Gibson City, took the witness stand and testified to the same regarding the farmland Hollman said he owned in Wisconsin.

Hollman had stayed at the Walters home and expressed a desire to provide reimbursement for the accommodation.

"He said he would come back and do a little work to pay me," Walters said. "He talked about chickens and said he was going to husk corn a month and then buy chickens."

Walters said Hollman took two small drinks from the half-gallon jug of whiskey. Walters claim he, himself, was not intoxicated.

"He started north from this place when he left," Walters added.

Katie Walters took the witness stand and testified she had seen Hollman last that Monday night of November 30th when he stayed at her home.

"He ate supper, played cards and drank whiskey there," Katie Walters said. "He exhibited two watches, one a lady's gold watch, the other a silvering watch. He talked in high German to me and my husband about shucking corn."

Katie Walters added that Hollman attracted her attention because "he was ugly."

Kevin Collier

Testimony at trial resumed on the morning of Tuesday, April 13. Among the witnesses were Harvey Bainter, Claus and Kate Hanson and Sheriff Benjamin Mason, whose testimony was most anticipated.

Harvey Bainter Testifies

Harvey Bainter, of Gibson City, was the first witness to take the stand.

Bainter testified he was at work for Hank Stuhmer when Frederick Hollman came to the Stuhmer farm looking for work just before noon the day of the Wiebke Geddes' murder. Bainter recalled the man was hired on the spot.

Bainter said Hollman was employed there until Sunday, with the exception of one day.

He recalled when he met Hollman he noticed marks on his chin. Bainter described the scratch on his chin as "pretty bad, about one-fourth of an inch long."

"It was a heavy scratch," Bainter said, adding "the skin was torn off" and the mark looked like it had been caused be fingernails.

"He had tooth-ache and his face was swollen. It attracted my attention," Bainter said, pointing out that at that moment "I had heard of Mrs. Geddes' death."

Bainter recalled Hollman was present the moment his step-brother, William Guise, arrived at the farm and announced the death of Wiebke Geddes.

Guise had heard the news while in town earlier.

Bainter said Hollman "looked down" when he heard the news.

117

Claus Hanson Testifies

Claus Hanson, residing four and a half miles southwest of the village of Melvin, took the witness stand and testified he and his wife Kate knew Fred Geddes and his late wife for about seven years dating back to their days in Germany.

"They lived in my house, up stairs, about five and a half months," Hanson recalled of the time the Geddes' arrived in America two years ago. "I never knew of them having a quarrel," he said.

Attention turned to identification of Fred Geddes' shaving razor, which was claimed to have been seen in Hollman's possession.

"Lots of times I saw Mr. Geddes's razor," Hanson stated. "I have shaved with it six or seven times."

While the item was missing, and not presented in evidence, Hanson described the razor in detail and noted the name "Sollingen" on object.

The witness said he never saw Hollman at or in his house. His wife, Kate had, but not he. Hanson explained that he had encountered Hollman at work at the Stuhmer farm.

"He came up to me in the field the Friday after the murder," Hanson recalled. "He came over to borrow the wagon."

Hanson said he noticed a scratch on the left side of Hollman's face and on his chin at the moment.

"He (Hollman) told me about the woman that was killed," Hanson said. "He said that the woman's husband had killed her."

Hanson thought Hollman's interest in the death to be somewhat unusual.

"I asked him if he (Fred Geddes) had hanged her on the door knob like (in) those others," Hanson said, in reference to the deaths of Grethe Seifkin and Carrie Lenz.

Hanson said Hollman changed the subject and expressed a goal. "He wanted to buy a (horse) team."

Kate Hanson Testifies

Kate Hanson, wife of Claus Hanson, took the witness stand and testified she had encountered Frederick Hollman three times.

The first time was at her home on Monday, November 30 after Carrie Lenz was murdered.

Kate Hanson said Hollman inquired where Hank Stuhmer lived, as he wanted to go there and shuck corn.

The second time she encountered Hollman was on Thursday, December 3, the day after Wiebke Geddes was murdered.

"I was on the porch alone. He went in the house with me," she recalled. "He said Fred Geddes struck his wife dead with a potato fork. I said, 'I don't believe it.' He said, 'But he did do it.'"

Kate Hanson said that Hollman explained that Fred Geddes had "tried to get away with the deed" but his own daughter had incriminated him and said he had committed the act.

While there, Kate Hanson said Hollman attempted to sell her a ladies' gold watch. Hollman claimed he had paid $20 for it in Chicago.

Hanson declined the offer, saying she had "no money" to purchase it.

The third time Kate Hanson encountered Hollman is when he returned briefly to Hanson's home on the morning of Friday, December 4 between 8:30 and 9:00.

Hanson said Hollman and she had discussed "tramps" that were said to be about, which was why she had locked the doors of her home.

"I told him that they (tramps) had stayed at the schoolhouse," Hanson said.

She recalled Hollman then showed her a shaving razor he had on his person, which she recognized as one belonging to Fred Geddes.

Kate Hanson relayed during her brief conversation with Hollman "he spoke about women as bad things."

Hollman asked how many children the Hansons had And Mrs. Hanson replied. Then Hollman stated he had a boy in Wisconsin who was 6 years old, and a girl born earlier.

Hollman then left the Hanson house.

Kate Hanson basically repeated what her husband had said in regards to the Geddes marriage, that Fred Geddes and his wife lived happily.

She added that the razor Hollman showed her that Friday had to have been the one owned by Fred Geddes.

"I heard my husband and Fred Geddes talk about the name 'Sollingen' on the razor when they (the Geddes) were (living) with us in the winter about two years ago," she added.

William Guise and Matthew Kerber Testify

William Guise took the witness stand and testified he had lived in Gibson City for about three years. He said was employed at the Stuhmer farm on when Hollman was hired on December 2.

Wiebke Geddes had been murdered that morning and Guise found out about it when he had run into town on an errand.

"I ate (an early) dinner with him (Hollman) that day," Guise said. "I noticed scar near ear. I spoke about the murder of Mrs. Geddes, and he (Hollman) hung his head and said nothing."

Guise said he overheard Hollman talking about "buying chickens," and that they shared a room together at the Stuhmer farmhouse.

Matthew Kerber took the witness stand next and noted the defendant left the farm Wednesday, December 2 after hearing about the Geddes murder and did not return until around noon that Friday, December 4.

Matthew Kerber testified he was employed at the Stuhmer farm and was present when Hollman was arrested on the early evening of December 6.

Kerber said he attended the funeral of Wiebke Geddes on Friday and upon returning to the Stuhmer farm spoke to Hollman about a conversation he overheard there at the service.

"I mentioned the fact that (others had talked about) a 'chicken peddler' that had been around," Kerber said.

Hollman appeared disturbed and rose from the dinner table.

"When the he got up, he rubbed his face and I could see a broad, tapering mark, three-fourths of an inch wide, plainly," Kerber said, acknowledging a wound on the man's face. "It was of a reddish-brown color. There was no scab."

Sheriff Benjamin F. Mason Testifies

Benjamin Franklin Mason, Sheriff of Ford County, took the witness stand and testified that he first saw Frederick Hollman in Gibson City during the Grand Jury inquest on the morning of December 7.

Hollman had been brought to the jailhouse the evening of December 6 by Constable Ira Gilmore, but Mason was not present at the time.

Mason said after Hollman was charged with murder, he took him into custody and brought him to Paxton and lodged him in jail.

Mason added that he did not notice the scratches on Hollman's face until two or three days after, when he had the man shaved.

"A finger nail would have made a scratch like it," Mason said. "Dr. (John Wesley) Reed (a dentist) noticed the marks. He

Kevin Collier

looked at it when he examined defendant and pulled two old stubs of teeth."

"His teeth were ulcerated and his face swollen," Mason added. "The mark just below his lower lip might have been made with any wide object," Mason said. He then questioned about Hollman's wounds.

Mason recalled Columbus Schneider saw a "a scratch or two" on Hollman's face "a day or two afterwards."

Mason interrogated Hollman at the jail and said the defendant claimed he had never offered to buy chickens from anyone as he "had no money to buy chickens with."

Mason relayed at first Hollman denied he had stayed at the Ashley schoolhouse, which was located three miles east of the Geddes residence.

Mason testified he reminded Hollman the key to the school and tiny mirror owned by teacher Jilian Johnson were found in his pocket when arrested by Constable Ira Gilmore. Mason said Hollman then admitted he had slept overnight at the school, but said he found the mirror in Waukegan, Illinois and picked up the key, which he said he found on the ground, by the railroad tracks in Bloomington.

It was revealed that Sheriff Mason had made an effort to find the missing shaving razor reportedly owned by Fred Geddes.

Mason said Hollman "could have owned" a razor, which was similar to the one owned by Fred Geddes.

"I made a visit to Waukegan (where Hollman said he had lived) and did not find the razor," Mason explained. "People (I spoke to) there who had seen Hollman (in Waukegan) had nothing (bad) to say against him."

Testimony at trial resumed on the morning of Wednesday, April 14. Among the witnesses were several individuals who saw Hollman running on the morning Wiebke Geddes was murdered, as well as John and Mattie Bushman, whose residence Hollman stayed at the night after the murder. Testimony also included information of Hollman sleeping at the schoolhouse.

Julius Lenz Testifies

Julius Lenz, age 30, half-brother of Albert Lenz whose wife Carrie was murdered on Thanksgiving Day, 1896 took the witness stand.

Lenz said he saw a man "come out of a corn field" on that day his sister-in-law was killed.

Julius Lenz explained for the jury Albert Lenz lived in Iroquois county, one-half mile south and two and one-half miles east of Danforth. Julius Lenz said he lived two miles east of that residence.

"It was the defendant," Lenz said, point to Hollman in the courtroom.

Lenz recalled he had visited the Ford County jail after Hollman's arrest to see if it was the same man he had seen the morning of his sister-in-law's death.

"I saw him in jail and recognized him as the party I saw on that day. Am sure it was him," Lenz stated. "He passed close to me and I called to him (that day) as I passed by me."

The testimony was delivered to establish Hollman was in that vicinity at the time, not to establish whether he had been the man who had killed Carrie Lenz.

Kevin Collier

Boarding House Owner John L. Maroney Testifies

John L. Maroney, former Hollman employer and owner of a boarding house in Bloomington, took the witness stand and testified he knew the defendant and that Hollman had first lived at the boarding house sometime in 1894.

"I live in Bloomington and keep a saloon and boarding house in connection with it," Maroney said. "I first saw him at my boarding house where he stayed for about three months."

Maroney also testified Hollman had worked for him doing odd jobs to earn his board.

He said he next saw Hollman in about May 1895.

After that, the next time he saw Hollman was when stayed the night of November 26 and 27, 1896.

"He stayed there Thursday and Friday night," Maroney said.

November 26 had been the day Carrie Lenz was murdered.

Prosecutor Abraham Phillips questioned Maroney if Hollman had shown him a woman's watch at that time.

"Yes. The one he had was a lady's watch, about the size of a dollar, possibly little larger," Maroney replied.

Phillips told the jury evidence supported that Hollman then gave the other watch, a gold one stolen from the Lenz residence, to Eliza C. Campbell, a woman he was fond of in Bloomington. Phillips said the watch had been given "as a gift."

John and Mattie Bushman Testify

John Bushman, who lived two and a half miles west of Guthrie in Ford County with his wife Mattie, took the witness stand and testified that he first met Hollman when he had worked for him in February 1896 cutting firewood.

He relayed the next time he saw the Hollman was Saturday, November 28, 1896.

"He said he came down from northern part of Wisconsin. He stayed with us until Monday morning," Bushman recalled.

"He told my wife that his feet were sore from walking. He showed us a gold watch about as large as a dollar. I asked him to let me see it, but he put it back in his pocket," Bushman added.

He said Hollman told him he owned 80 acres of land in Wisconsin. Bushman said Hollman told him he had arrived in America from Brandenburg, Germany.

Prosecutor Phillips asked Bushman if Hollman had spoken about any women.

"He said if he found a widow that wanted to marry he wanted one," Bushman replied.

Mattie Bushman took the witness stand next and confirmed what her husband had said concerning how they first met Hollman.

She added information concerning their second encounter with Hollman on November 28.

"He said walked in from north, asked for a slop pail to put his feet in, they were blistered," Mattie Bushman said.

"He showed me a hunting case, a stem winder watch and an engraved case," Bushman said. She explained Hollman told her he got the watch in Chicago for two dollars.

Mrs. Bushman said Hollman showed her "the watch" a number of times. She also noticed that there scratches on his chin.

"He said he was going to buy chickens in the spring. He wanted to form a partnership with me and buy chickens," Bushman added. She also said Hollman talked about women.

Hollman stayed overnight Saturday and Sunday and left about 10 or 10:30 in the morning on Monday, November 30.

Hollman returned to their house on Thursday, December 3, the day after the murder of Wiebke Geddes and stayed the night.

The defendant brought up the murder and had said of Fred Geddes "the pig had killed his wife." Kate Hanson told Hollman she did not believe Fred Geddes had committed the act, and said he replied, "The little girl had said her father had killed her mother."

Prosecutor Phillips attempted to show Hollman, who had worked for the Bushmans in February 1896, was in the area when Grethe Seifkin was murdered. Seifkin, who lived near Melvin, was killed on June 13, 1896.

Regarding that, Kate Bushman said Hollman told her he had left this part of the state in May 1896.

Student Julius C. Heckens Testifies

Ashley School student Julius C. Heckens, age 12, took the witness stand and recalled he had met a stranger in the road about one-half mile from the Ashley schoolhouse on December 1 between 4 and 5:00 in the afternoon.

The boy lived with his parents Claus and Mary Heckens three and a half miles north of Gibson City, a little southwest of Garber.

The school was one half mile south and mile west.

He said his teacher was Miss Lilian Johnson.

Heckens explained he was headed home from school with his brother, Peter. He identified Hollman in the courtroom as the man he saw on foot that day, who was headed west.

"My little 5-year-old brother was with me," Heckens said. "I did not notice where defendant went after I passed him, nor did I notice any scratches on his face."

Heckens did say the man "was going in the direction of the schoolhouse."

He recalled that when he went make a fire in the woodstove at the schoolhouse the next morning, on December 2 at a little past 8:00, he found one already lit.

"There was a fire already there burning," Heckens said. "And the schoolhouse key was missing."

Teacher Lilian Johnson Testifies

Ashley school teacher Miss Lilian Johnson, who lived 3 miles north of Gibson City, took the witness stand.

Johnson taught school the day Wiebke Geddes was found murdered. She noted her chair was not at her desk.

"On the morning of December 2, when I went to school, my chair was down by the woodstove. One bench was disturbed, as well," Johnson said.

Prosecutor Abraham Phillips showed Lilian Johnson the key recovered from Hollman's pocket when he was arrested. She positively identified the key as belonging to the schoolhouse by the "No. 1" engraved into it.

She also confirmed that a small hand mirror she owned which was missing. She identified the mirror as the one that had been found in Hollman's possession.

John Stroh, Jr. Recalled to Stand

John Stroh, Jr. retook the witness stand and explained he lived at the home of his parents on their farm.

He stated that on morning of December 2, 1896, he was riding in a wagon on the way to the cornfield to work.

"I was on the wagon with my sister Minnie, aged 18," Stroh said. "We all went to the cornfield together that morning. We were ahead, Fred Geddes was following us. About 6:00 I saw a man running."

He estimated the man running through the field was 220 yards away.

"My sister said, 'What is that?' I said, Maybe it is a tramp," he recalled.

Kevin Collier

Testimony at trial resumed on the morning of Thursday, April 15. Among the witnesses were Hank Stuhmer, son of the farm owner, and Henry Selberg, who encountered Hollman on the morning Wiebke Geddes was murdered. Also, several witnesses who had testified earlier were recalled. Louise Stuhmer, wife of Hank Stuhmer testified in regards to finding what was believed to be Fred Geddes' stolen shaving razor on the floor of the farmhouse kitchen. Doctors were recalled to give further testimony on the wounds found on Hollman's face.

Newspapers reported two women living near Sibley testified about Hollman calling at their houses on the day before Wiebke Geddes was murdered, but what was said at the courtroom was not documented. Newspapers did not report the names of the women. It is likely one of the two was Sophia (Heinrichs) Hendricks, neighbor of Grethe Seifkin.

Frederick Hollman would also take the stand, much to the disapproval of his defense attorney Columbus Schneider.

Hank Stuhmer Testifies

Hank Stuhmer, son of the Stuhmer farm owner, took the witness stand and testified the witnessed Hollman on December 2, 1896 near the Ashley schoolhouse.

"I was going to Sibley in a one-seated buggy," Stuhmer recalled. "I live a mile west of the Ashley schoolhouse." Stuhmer explained he spotted Hollman 110 to 165 yards up ahead coming through a hedge along the road.

"The road runs east and west and the defendant was in the road ahead of me," Stuhmer recalled. "I recollect there was a stalk or cornfield where he went through the hedge."

Defense attorney Columbus Schneider strongly pointed to the hedge as being the source of his client's facial scratches.

Stuhmer said he and Hollman exchanged words, then parted ways.

"I saw the man just a mile from the schoolhouse where I turned."

Henry Selberg Testifies

Henry (Herman) Selberg took the witness stand and explained he originally lived in Minnesota but had resided in the area about one year prior to the murder of Wiebke Geddes.

"I farmed 170 acres at the Zimmerman place and husked corn in the field east of the pasture on the morning of December 2, 1896," Selberg recalled.

It was about 7:30 when Selberg, who was husking corn, encountered Hollman along the road.

"When I first noticed him, my horses raised their heads," Selberg said. The witness recalled he noticed fresh blood on the man's chin.

"I looked up and he came towards me. I said, 'Good morning.' He walked behind me quite a long way on the left side while I husked corn." Selberg said. "I did not see his hands. He had his hands in his overcoat pockets. I felt kind of nervous."

Selberg explained that he asked the man where he had come from and he said Hollman replied that he arrived "from the north" and had "recently been in Melvin."

"He wanted to know where Hank Stuhmer lived," Selberg recalled. "I told him the best I could. Then, he then left me."

On cross-examination, Columbus Schneider pressed Selberg on Hollman's wounds and them being a result of passing through the hedge.

Schneider asked Selberg that if the scratches had been caused earlier, would not Hollman have washed the blood from his face?

"The hedge where he came in is thin in some places and thick in others," Selberg recalled. "There was a ditch along the road where the blood could have been washed off. It was about twenty feet further east."

Selberg, on his way to work at the time, said Hollman followed him for about 10 yards.

"He did not talk nor help me shuck. It seemed to be fresh blood. Saw it when he first came up. He made no attempt to hide it," Selburg explained. "He seemed anxious to know where Hank Stuhmer lived and as soon as I told him and went south to the road."

Selberg also noted had he saw no one else pass on the road earlier that morning.

James Grant Testifies

James Grant took the witness stand and noted he lived in Gibson City. On December 2, 1896 he was hauling gravel from Robert McClure's gravel pit to the Stuhmer farm.

"One mile south and two and a half miles west, I met a man," Grant testified. "He rode to the Melvin corner, then went north to the road. He told me he was going to Hank Stuhmer's to see about shucking corn."

Grant described the garments the man wore.

"It was a dark gray overcoat and cap," Grant said.

But Grant admitted he was not sure the man before him the courtroom, Frederick Hollman, was this man.

"I cannot say positively that this is the man," he said.

Hank Stuhmer Recalled to Stand

Hank Stuhmer was put back on the witness stand for lengthy, additional testimony.

Prosecutor Phillips focused on Hollman's arrival at the Stuhmer farm around 11:45 the morning of Wiebke Geddes' death, December 2, 1896.

"When I got back from Sibley on the morning of the Geddes murder this fellow Hartman (Hollman) and another fellow were at my house," Stuhmer recalled.

"Hartman and I shucked in the same wagon. He asked me what was that fellow's name was who worked for Stroh. I said it was Fred Geddes." Stuhmer and the farm workers noticed the marks on Hollman's face.

Stuhmer explained after the topic of Geddes came up that Hollman became anxious and departed to get a team of horses over at John Phillips' farm as workmen went out into the field.

"He did not say what time he would be back," Stuhmer recalled.

When Hollman did not return, Stuhmer imagined he would be back by noon on the next day, December 3.

"We were sitting at the table talking about him and saying we did not look for him to come back," Stuhmer recalled that evening.

Hollman returned the following day, on Friday, December 4.

"He had a black mark on his forehead. I paid him and he started off (into the cornfield)," Stuhmer said.

Hollman was accompanied by two other workmen and a team of horses.

"I let him husk by himself and paid him 2 cents a bushel," Stuhmer said. "He husked from Friday noon until Saturday night." Stuhmer recalled. "One of the boys (farm hands) said he (Hollman) acted so funny (amusing) we ought to keep him."

Stuhmer then testified as to the conduct of Hollman at the farmhouse up to the time of his arrest. He told of Hollman's hostile about women in general, toward whom he seemed to have "an antipathy."

August Myer Testifies

August Myer, a 36-year-old farm hand, took the witness stand and testified he lived three-quarters of a mile from the Stuhmer farmhouse and was husking corn on the farm Sunday afternoon, December 6, 1896.

August Myer stated that he frequently worked for the Stuhmers.

Myer stated he had been at the home of Chris Walters when they had discussed the gold women's wrist watch Hollman had been flashing around. He said he had made attempts to try to identify it.

Myer explained that he spoke to Frederick Hollman that weekend about the murder of Wiebke Geddes. He said Hollman told him that her husband, Fred Geddes, had committed the crime. Myer informed Hollman that authorities had released Fred Geddes from jail and no longer considered him a suspect.

Myer said he then told Hollman "it was a chicken peddler that did it."

Hollman responded that if it was a chicken peddler the man would be long gone by now, "in Chicago or further off."

"I told him no," Myer recalled. "He is right in our neighborhood, not gone away."

Myer explained Hollman's posture upon hearing this was "cast down" and he appeared "pale in color."

He recalled that he thought Hollman's reaction was suspicious, and that he would leave after hearing what he said, but surprisingly, Hollman stayed at the Stuhmer farm.

Myer also noticed a scar on the defendant's chin at the time.

Louise Stuhmer Testifies

Louise Stuhmer, wife of Hank Stuhmer, took the witness stand and testified she had visited the Geddes family at their home "four or five times" and they were a happily married, "pleasant couple."

She recalled Frederick Hollman showing up for work at their farmhouse between 10:00-11:00 the morning of December 2, 1896.

"He (Hollman) sat there in the house until my husband (Hank) came in," Louise Stuhmer recalled.

While alone, she said Hollman asked if she had any chickens to sell, as he could offer a good price. Stuhmer said she told Hollman she had already sold all the chickens she had.

Louise Stuhmer recalled Hollman talked briefly about women, and "evenings with them."

Hollman was hired on, went out with the men to husk corn, and came in and sat down for lunch with the men. When the talk at the table turned to the murder of Wiebke Geddes, "he (Hollman) became uncomfortable," Stuhmer said.

She recalled that when Hollman went back out into the field after lunch, he did not return to work until two days later on Friday, December 4.

Stuhmer recalled two other men left employment at the farm about the time Hollman did, one identified as Henry Daman, and another man whose identity was unknown. But Stuhmer said the unknown individual was a heavy-set man, and older than Hollman.

However, according to Louise Stuhmer, he bore a resemblance to Hollman and even wore a "scotch cap" similar to the one owned by the accused.

Another man named Henry Harvey had hung his coat in the farmhouse kitchen beside Hollman's, but continued employment there.

Louise Stuhmer said that after Hollman's departed for the day, she found a men's shaving razor that afternoon of December 2, which during the Geddes murder investigation matched the description of the one stolen from the Geddes home. Hollman had put on another coat he owned when he departed leaving a larger overcoat behind in the kitchen. He would not return to the farmhouse until December 4.

Defense attorney Columbus Schneider interrupted and cross-examined the witness.

During Schneider's questioning, Stuhmer admitted she had not discovered the razor in Hollman's pocket but instead found it resting upon the kitchen floor. Children had been playing in the coats of the workmen and they had fallen to the floor. Louise Stuhmer said she picked up the razor and put it into Hollman's coat pocket assuming it was his.

A coat similar to Hollman's dark gray overcoat was hanging in the kitchen, too, but was said to be black Stuhmer recalled, and owned by the "heavy-set" older man that also departed that afternoon and who likewise did not return.

Columbus Schneider played on this to place doubt in the minds of the jurors.

No one could recall the other man's name, who was said to resemble Hollman and wore a similar coat and scotch cap.

"I have never heard anything about the man since," Mrs. Stuhmer said, admitting the stranger's anonymity.

Louise Stuhmer perfectly described the "Sollingen" razor, right down to its broken case.

She said she took the razor out of Hollman's coat pocket later get a better look at it, then told her husband.

Stuhmer admitted she would not know a shaving razor was missing from the Geddes home until speaking with Geddes the evening of December 6 when Hollman was arrested.

However, Stuhmer testified she suspecting Hollman might be the killer of Wiebke Geddes. She had moved the Hollman's coat to a front first level room so she could observe whether Hollman would reach into his pocket to retrieve a razor.

"I was afraid he might hurt us," she said.

Louise Stuhmer testified she informed Hollman she had moved his coat "because the children played in the kitchen" and had knocked the workmen's coats down.

Stuhmer said she asked Hollman about a razor, but conveyed he had nothing to say about it.

Stuhmer then said she asked Constable Ira Gilmore when Hollman was arrested at the farmhouse if he had found the razor. Gilmore told the woman he had not.

Columbus Schneider asked Louise Stuhmer a series of questions to raise doubt in the minds of the jurors about whether Hollman ever had a razor in his possession.

Q: Didn't he (the unnamed man) and Hollman, during lunch, hang their coats there?

A: I do not know. I first saw the razor on the floor in the afternoon.

Q: Then you didn't take it out of this man's (pointing to Hollman) pocket?

A: No, not then.

Q: I asked you if you found it (the razor) on the floor.

A: Yes.

Q: Then, you don't know whether it was in the pocket (of Hollman's coat) or not?

A: I didn't see the razor before the kids tore down the coats. Then, I saw the razor.

Prosecuting attorney Abraham Phillips objected, believing the witness was being harassed. Schneider heeded warning from Judge Sample and continued with caution.

Q: You don't know whether they (the kids) got it (the razor) from the coat or somewhere else?

A: No.

Louise Stuhmer admitted when she told her husband Hank about the razor he said "that was nothing" and dismissed it.

She also admitted the issue of the razor (a being a piece of evidence) did not transpire until after Hollman was arrested and taken to jail. So, while Louise Stuhmer suspected something, at that time she did not know if the item was stolen or if it even belonged to Fred Geddes.

Wilkinson, Geddes, Stroh and Houdyshell Testify

23-year-old photographer Edward Wilkinson took the witness stand and testified in regards to photos he had taken of the Geddes home after shrubs obscuring the kitchen windows had been recently removed.

The testimony was an attempt to prove that the Stroh family had removed brush that would have hidden a murderer inside the dwelling.

Fred Geddes was briefly recalled to testify that the photos presented were indeed of his home.

John Stroh, Jr. was recalled to testify that he saw Hollman hiding under the bed sheets when arrested in the upstairs bedroom at the Stuhmer farmhouse on December 6, 1896.

Charles Houdyshell was recalled to explain Hollman's transport to Gibson City after his arrest, and a conversation the two had.

Doctors Cutler, Reed and Lovell Testify

Doctor Frank O. Cutler was recalled to testify. Cutler described the wounds on Hollman's face and thought "three layers of skin" had been scratched away causing the scab. He explained Wiebke Geddes' fingernails were "neatly trimmed" but contained blood evidence and bits of flesh from another person.

Dentist John Wesley Reed testified as to the wound on Hollman' face and explained he had extracted two teeth from the defendant after he was lodged in the Ford County jail. He thought the marks on Hollman's face were "scratches" caused by someone's fingernails.

"A fingernail held right would possibly make such a mark at that on the face, depending on the angle," he stated.

Doctor Frank B. Lovell, a graduate of Rush Medical College and Bellevue Hospital, took the witness stand and testified that he knew Fred Geddes and his wife and that the couple made a good family and were attentive to the needs of their handicapped daughter Elizabeth. He added that he examined Hollman in Prosecutor Phillips' office soon after the arrest.

He observed "a welt or swollen streak" diagonally across the right side of the defendant's back from the ninth rib to the vertebra.

"He claimed it to be a birthmark," Lovell recalled. "He had a mark on his face he said was made by a briar which flew back and struck him when he was crawling through a hedge."

Lovell explained that the injury on Hollman's face "appeared to have been made with an instrument similar to a fingernail," and was one and a half inches in length.

"When I examined Hollman he seemed to be laboring under a great deal of excitement," Lovell said. "He was trembling in his lower limbs and constantly changed his position. When I undressed him he took hold of one of his lower limbs and said he had rheumatism."

Lovell testified Hollman mentioned he was robbed and been involved in a trial in Waukegan, Illinois. He also said Hollman claimed he never attempted to "buy chickens," as he had no money.

Cutler also said Hollman told him that he knew the Lenz family, as he had worked for them at one time.

The doctor reported that during his examination of Hollman, it appeared as if the front of his shirt "had been washed."

An attempt was made to establish a timeline to better determine when Wiebke Geddes had actually died. Lovell explained that rigor mortis can take longer to set in under cold (winter) circumstances, indicating she might have been killed later the morning of December 2.

Schroeder, Jensen, Preston, Johnson and Grim Testify

25-year-old Emma Schroeder took the witness stand and testified that Frederick Hollman arrived at her home between 3:00-4:00 on the afternoon of December 1, 1896, a day before the Geddes murder.

Schroeder explained that Hollman was looking for a place to stay. She told him they had no room. According to Schroeder, the two talked briefly about her children, then he departed, heading to the Katherina Jensen residence.

Katherina Jensen took the witness stand and testified she had encountered Hollman, who was still looking for a place to stay between 4:00-5:00 that same afternoon. The 73-year-old widow explained she lived in the residence of her widowed daughter Mary M. Borchers and two grandsons.

"He (Hollman) came in the house and wanted to stay overnight," Jensen said. "I was alone at the time, and told him he could not stay." Schroeder stated Hollman then departed.

Gibson City Justice of the Peace Jacob W. Preston took the witness stand and testified he was present when Hollman was physically examined and witnessed the welt on his back and the scratches on his face.

Samuel Johnson, a city Marshall of Gibson City took the witness stand and testified he saw Hollman late Sunday night, the day of his arrest. He also described Hollman's facial wounds.

Miss Mary Grim, a stenographer present during Hollman's initial questioning by attorney Abraham Phillips, corroborated what was asked and said. This authenticated and placed on record the answers Hollman gave during his initial interrogation.

Gilmore, Selberg, Mason, Lovell, Reno and Others Testify

Constable Ira Gilmore took the witness stand and recalled for the jury the day he arrested Hollman at the Stuhmer farmhouse. Gilmore corroborated earlier witness testimony regarding that event.

Gilmore identified the pocketbook, the money it contained, the key to the schoolhouse and silver watch with chain. He had seized all of these items from Hollman's possession upon a search when he was arrested. He said Hollman claimed he found the key on the railroad tracks in Bloomington.

The Constable said he noticed the marks on Hollman's face and back when examining him and recalled that at least twenty to thirty people had gathered at the farmhouse the evening of December 6, 1896 to guard against the suspect fleeing.

Gilmore said that when he confronted Hollman in the upstairs bedroom of the home he was hiding under a sheet on his bed tick. "When I pulled the cover off him in bed," Gilmore recalled, "he said, 'There, you have got that all wrong, you have got the wrong man.'"

Gilmore stated he put Hollman in handcuffs as the search for evidence was conducted and brought him to Gibson City to be examined and jailed.

Albert Selberg, age 16 and younger brother of Henry Selberg, took the witness stand and testified that he was present at the Stuhmer farmhouse the evening of Hollman's arrest.

Selberg said he heard Louise Stuhmer ask the police if they had "found the razor" in Hollman's possession.

Defense attorney Columbus Schnieder asked Selberg if he heard a reply from Mrs. Stuhmer.

"He (Hollman) said he had one in his trunk (he left back) in Waukegan," Selberg recalled. "That's the first I heard of a razor."

Sheriff Benjamin Mason was recalled to the stand and gave additional testimony regarding evidence exhibited at trial.

Mason said they had not found a gold watch on Hollman during a search after his arrest. He said he noticed the scratch on Hollman's face, which became more visible to others, once the defendant was shaven soon after he was jailed.

Mason recalled that Hollman's tooth was pulled on December 9 or 10 and that he had complained about having a back pain around the same time.

Schnieder then questioned Mason about the mirror that reportedly belonged to Ashley school teacher Lilian Johnson.

Q: You did not say what you did with the looking glass?

A: I took it away from Hollman (after he was apprehended) and looked at it, then gave it back to him.

Q: You gave it back to the defendant?

A: I found out where the glass belonged when my men went out to the school to see if the key fitted the schoolhouse. (It was then) Miss Johnson said (to officers) her looking glass was missing. I want to correct the statement I made the other day regarding the looking glass. I took it off Hollman in jail, then after receiving a telegram (took it) to get (into evidence) the looking glass.

David Reno, a 34-year-old farmer, next took the witness stand and testified he lived two and a half miles west of the Geddes' home. Reno identified Hollman as the man that was "presenting (himself) to buy chickens." Reno said he saw Hollman passing by the Geddes house and seen west of the Brandt's home on the north and south roads.

"He wanted to buy chickens from me," Reno recalled. "He said he was paying eight cents a pound, and they were shipped to Joliet. He told me he spoke with (Wiebke) Geddes and said he was paying too much rent for the house."

Reno relayed this occurred around the time Wiebke Geddes was murdered, but could not pinpoint the day.

Reno said Hollman had indicated that he had stopped at the home of Matthew Kerber and had stayed at his home for only 30 minutes.

Hank Stuhmer and Fred Geddes retook the witness stand briefly and both stated the name brand on the missing shaving razor was "Sollengen."

Sheriff Mason was briefly recalled and asked as to the defendant's true name as he knew it. While Hollman used the name of Hartman when arrested Mason said that in time, "the name given by the defendant in jail was Frederick Hollman."

Doctor Frank Lovell was recalled to the witness stand again to testify as to Hollman's examination.

Doctor J. Mahan took the witness stand and briefly testified as to the effect a blow by the spading fork would have on the inner membrane of a human brain.

The prosecution then rested.

Kevin Collier

Hollman's defense attorney, Columbus Schneider, now put several witnesses on the stand to clarify details of their testimony.

Coroner William A. Hutchison testified as to the initial inquest into the death of Wiebke Geddes and his findings concluding that Fred Geddes had killed his wife.

Fred W. Beardsley, a member of the inquest jury, as well as Fred Geddes, were recalled to give clarifying testimony.

Doctor Frank O. Cutler took the witness stand once again and described the condition of Wiebke Geddes' body at the murder scene.

Constable Ira Gilmore testified in regards to the search made with bloodhounds to find the missing shaving razor and gold watch discussed at trial.

Lena Timmons and Isaac H. Bond both took the witness stand, but neither knew anything of importance. Hollman reportedly had approached both men seeking work at one time.

Johanna Voss, the daughter of Michael and Margaret Voss, testified that she was present at the inquest naming Fred Geddes as the killer and explained she had acted as the interpreter of Elizabeth Geddes for authorities.

John Zimmerman and his wife Sarah took the witness stand and testified Hollman had stopped at their farm on December 1, 1896 seeking work. They recalled they gave him something to eat, then sent him on to the Hansen home. The couple recalled Hollman said he "had no money." The Zimmermans said they saw no wounds on Hollman's face at the time.

Kevin Collier

During the trial it was reported Frederick Hollman asked Sheriff Mason for a pistol in order that he might "kill the jurors." It is unknown if he made this request in private or at trial before the jurors. But it had become clear to his defense attorney Columbus Schneider, if Hollman took the witness stand, he would likely hang himself.

During the week's testimony, Hollman often interjected making damaging remarks. Judge Sample admonished Hollman for this and Schneider kept a constant watch of his client often using persuasion to prevent further outbursts.

Hollman ignored the objection of Schneider on taking the witness stand to testify on his own behalf. Schneider believed Hollman would only further incriminate himself.

"Schneider tried to keep Hollman off the stand, but he was determined to testify," The Pantagraph newspaper reported.

Hollman took the stand and was questioned "for many hours," the Gibson City Courier reported.

The initial questions were presented by his defense attorney and were an attempt to educate the jury as to whom his client was.

"My correct name Frederich Wilhelm Hoellman," Hollman began. "I changed my name when I left my second wife in Wisconsin. I am 38-years-old, and was born in the little village of Leonars in the northern part of Brandenburg, Germany. I lived in Brandenburg until 1883 when I came over the sea and to Michigan with my wife Amelia Cards."

Hollman then assumed a somber mood.

"We had two children," he said. "My wife lived until 1887. On the ninth day of the following August, I again married and had two children by my second wife, Augusta Rhode."

Schneider asked Hollman as to the whereabouts of his wife, of which the jury was curious.

"My second wife lives between Dartford and Ripon, Wisconsin," Hollman replied. "I have never seen her since I left her five years ago."

Hollman said he had tried get financial assistance for his defense from his brother Julius and his cousin Charlie but neither contributed.

"I have a cousin (Charlie) living in Grand Haven, Michigan, and a brother (Julius) in Wisconsin," Hollman said. "But, I was unable to reach them by letter."

Defense attorney Schneider then tried to establish Hollman's whereabouts for the jury from November 26, 1896 to the time of his arrest on December 6.

Hollman claimed he stayed at the Walsh home in Bloomington on the night of November 26, 1896, the day Carrie Lenz was murdered in Gilman. Prior to that, he said he had been around Kenosha, Wisconsin since the first days of June 1896.

Hollman said he had arrived in Bloomington by train that evening of November 26, 1896 and remained there until Saturday, November 28. He claimed that he took a train at around 8:00 the morning of November 28 and reached Gibson City around 10:00, then went to Melvin.

Hollman confirmed earlier testimony by John and Mattie Bushman that he stayed at their home that Saturday evening and departed their residence sometime the morning of November 30.

Hollman stated he stopped at John Brandt's home on November 30 and the man invited him in for lunch.

From there, Hollman said he went looking for work stopping at the Timmons farm, then called on Isaac H. Bond, and ended up at the residence of Claus Hanson.

It was around that time Hollman said he scratched his face when going through a hedge.

That evening, he said he stayed overnight at the home of Chris and Katie Walters, corroborating their testimony. He said they played cards and drank whiskey. Hollman said he left the Walter's place about 9:00 the morning of December 1.

Hollman claimed that while on his way to the Ashley schoolhouse he encountered a "chicken peddler," who asked him where a man lived from whom he wanted to buy some chickens.

He then testified that he went east to the Ashley schoolhouse around 5:00 in the afternoon and stayed there that night.

"I got up and fixed a fire in the schoolhouse, I think, right after 6:00 (the morning of December 2)," Hollman explained. "I washed my face at the schoolhouse pump and put the basin under the step (of the building.) I had a scratch on my face when I washed. I left the schoolhouse about a quarter past 7:00 and went north to hunt for a place to husk corn."

From there he said he encountered Henry Selberg, who was working on the Zimmerman farm, upon passing through a hedge on the road. Hollman stated Selberg said the Stuhmer farm was hiring corn huskers. After receiving directions, Hollman said he briefly spoke with Albert Selberg, Henry's brother, who was also working on the Zimmerman property. Hollman departed and went to the Stuhmer farmhouse, where he was hired around noon.

"I heard about the Geddes murder Wednesday night," Hollman said. "Bill Guise told me the man who worked for Stroh had killed his wife with a spading fork."

Hollman said he went to the Bushman's the next day, December 3, where he stayed the night, and departed there on Friday morning. He said he then returned to the Stuhmer farm to resume work there. He added he had hitched a ride from farm hand Hank Steh, who was driving a horse-drawn wagon. Hollman claimed he slipped and fell on the edge of the wagon box while riding, accounting for the bruising injury on his back.

Defense attorney Schneider then asked Hollman about his reaction during his arrest.

Q: Do you remember a crowd congregating out at the Stuhmer farm on Sunday, December 6?

A: Yes.

Q: Did you think it was strange that quite a number of persons were (gathered) there on Sunday afternoon?

A: Yes.

Schneider walked Hollman through his arrest at the Stuhmer farmhouse, which occurred around 8:00 that evening. Hollman said he had the blanket over his face when Constable Gilmore entered his bedroom because a window was broken and cold air was streaming indoors. He indicated he was "not hiding" from the lawman.

Columbus Schneider then surrendered his client for cross-examination and Prosecuting attorney Abraham Phillips approached Hollman.

Phillips began by questioning Hollman about changing his name after he left his second wife, Augusta.

Hollman claimed he did so in order to not be bothered by her.

The defendant was then asked to once again walk the jury through his identity and whereabouts.

Hollman stated again for the jury he was born in the town of Leonars in Brandenburg, Germany and outlined his life in Grand Haven, Michigan with his first wife Amelia. He explained they had two children, and they had all died by 1887.

He said he remarried the next year to the woman who was his current wife, August Pauline Hollman. They had two children. He noted he hadn't seen them "in over five years" since abandoning them.

Hollman then explained where he had worked and traveled since leaving his wife in January 1892, bringing the timeline up to the moment of his arrest on December 6, 1896.

Of note, during this testimony, Hollman's convenient timelines excluded him from the locations at the time several murders attributed to him had occurred.

Hollman stated he left Melvin, Illinois "on the first or second day of June 1896" and went to Waukegan, Illinois "where I worked nearly all summer long." Hollman added, "and people know that, too!"

Grethe Seifkin had been murdered on June 13, less than two weeks after Hollman said he had departed the area.

Prosecutor Phillips asked Hollman how he knew of the manner in which Grethe Seifkin had been murdered. Hollman said he was in Chenoa, nearly 30 miles away when it occurred, and that he did not know. Then he corrected himself and said he had traveled to Waukegan for the summer to find work.

However, evidence showed Hollman was not in Waukegan for the summer. He then admitted the error and placed himself in Pleasant Prairie, Wisconsin for most of that time.

Hollman stated he lived "for a month" at the home of farmer Henry Lang, who owned a farmhouse in Pleasant Prairie, Wisconsin.

This placed Hollman in the same location where Bertha Hilgendorf was murdered on July 4. This murder apparently was not disclosed during the trial because this woman's husband, August Hilgendorf, had been convicted of the crime and was in prison at Waupun.

Hollman then said that is when he went to Waukegan, Illinois.

However, eyewitnesses recalled Hollman leaving the area "a day after" Hilgendorf's death and not before talking to others about the tragedy telling them that "the man killed his wife."

Hollman said in August he traveled to Randolph, Illinois, near Bloomington, where he worked "until September 25th" placing him away from Wisconsin when Catherine Mohr was murdered on September 20, 1896. Prosecutor Phillips did not bring up Mohr, however, or that the woman resided in the town of Somers, Wisconsin, only a few miles north of Pleasant Prairie.

Hollman said he then went to work at the Forman farm in Bloomington the first part of October 1896 before he returned to Milwaukee and was hired there to shuck corn.

He claimed he was in Waukegan for six days when the first snow came, then returned to the area by train in Bloomington the evening of November 26.

Carrie Lenz had been murdered the morning of that same day.

Hollman incriminated himself in the death of Carrie Lenz when he became confused about dates and placed himself in "two or three miles east of Danforth" near Gilman in November 1896 working for farmer William Currie.

Defense attorney Columbus Schneider objected, and Hollman became excited and stuttered, aware of his error.

Hollman had earlier claimed that he stayed at the Walsh home in Bloomington on the evening of November 26, 1896 after arriving from Wisconsin by train. However, John L. Maroney, owner of a boarding house in Bloomington, testified Hollman had stayed at his establishment on the evening of November 26, 1896.

At this point, Hollman began to retrace his movements for Prosecutor Phillips, but this time placed the wounds on his face.

Hollman explained that after he visited John Bushman on November 27, the day after the death of Carrie Lenz, he ended up on the property of John Miner, and when going through a hedge bent back part of a stump that had recoiled back into his face.

"I bent it in, and that stump struck me right here on the right side of my face," Hollman testified. "I never denied that, either."

Phillips then challenged the defendant, knowing that now Hollman's facial wounds could not have existed when he stayed with Chris and Katie Walters for two nights the weekend before Wiebke Geddes was murdered.

Phillips asked Hollman why the couple reported seeing no scratches on his face at the time.

"They couldn't see anything like that," Hollman responded, with anger. "That woman (Katie) drinks as much whiskey, as he (Chris) does!"

Prosecutor Phillips reminded the jury it was pointed out in testimony delivered by farmer John Miner that no hedge existed on his property at the location Hollman said he had scratched his face.

Hollman then attempted to explain his whereabouts the two days before Wiebke Geddes was murdered, naming farmers he had approached asking for work.

Hollman traced his path to the Ashley schoolhouse and admitted he had met student Julius Heckens along the way, but did not recall his younger brother Peter in his company. Hollman said he exchanged no words with the children.

He next explained how he gained access into the schoolhouse, where he slept overnight until the early hours of December 2.

"Met a fellow (coming out of the school building) and just stepped back, until he passed," Hollman said. "Then (I) went in."

After outlining again how he had slept at the schoolhouse for the night Hollman claimed he departed around a quarter past 7:00. He said he then encountered Henry Selberg along the road about 10:00, and asked him where he could find work. Hollman explained Selberg recommended he try the Stuhmer farm and provided directions.

Phillips then asked Hollman several questions attempting to place him at the Geddes residence the morning of the murder.

Q: Isn't it a fact you went west from the schoolhouse that morning and went across to the Geddes house? Don't you know where the Geddes house is?

A: No, sir.

Q: Don't you know Mrs. Geddes?

A: I only saw her once, in the spring of 1896.

Q: Don't you know about a week before the murder you were at the Geddes house?

A: About a week? No.

Q: Didn't you tell someone Geddes was paying too much rent?

A: No, that is only made-up business against me.

A: Weren't you at the Voss home?

A: No, sir.

Q: Weren't you at the Geddes home?

A: No, sir.

Q: Weren't you at the Claus Stroh's place?

A: No, sir.

Q: Weren't you at David Reno's?

A: No, sir.

Q: Weren't you at the home of William Brandt?

A: When was that, in the spring?

Hollman had denied most everything and seemed overwhelmed at the moment.

Prosecutor Phillips questioned Hollman about posing as a chicken buyer, which ruffled the feathers of the accused.

Whereas Hollman dismissed the notion he was a "chicken buyer," he did acquiesce by saying a poultry place in Arrowsmith was shipping chickens to Joliet and had pitched the idea to him to inquire around about people who might have chickens to sell.

Phillips next focused on the large bruise found on Hollman's back at the time of his arrest on December 6, 1896.

Q: You say the welt on your back was due to falling on a wagon box?

A: I slipped and fell on the boards.

Q: You said that night (of your arrest) you didn't have any marks on you except a birthmark?

A: I have it yet, it comes from my kidneys.

Prosecutor Phillips stayed on the moment of Hollman's arrest and noted the accused said he had retired early on account of a toothache.

"The officer (Ira Gilmore) came in (to the bedroom) and pulled the sheet off me and said, 'Get up, and get your clothes on. I want you,'" Hollman recalled. "I said, you've got the wrong man."

Hollman stated prior to his arrest he had no idea he was considered a suspect in the death of Wiebke Geddes.

Hollman denied having been in possession of a ladies gold watch that morning, or a men's razor, and blasted the notion he had hidden them before his capture.

He denied ever showing a gold watch to John Maroney and stated he had sold a men's sold watch in Bloomington, one which he purchased in Chicago.

He then explained how the small mirror from the schoolhouse found on him came into his possession and how the key to the building did not come from that location, but he had found it near the railroad tracks in Bloomington.

"It appears you only fetch things up that don't belong to you?" Phillips commented for the jury.

Hollman denied he had two pocketbooks on him when he was arrested and stated he had never before seen the type of binding twine that was used to hang Wiebke Geddes and Carrie Lenz from door knobs.

Phillips then initiated a display of theatrics that jury found quite curious.

Phillips handed Hollman a piece of binding twine similar to the cord found tied around Mrs. Geddes' neck and the other victims and asked him if he could "tie a knot."

Hollman reportedly grinned, as one newspaper described, "in as quick as a flash" he tied the cord in a particular sailor's knot that matched the binding method used on the victims.

"There," Hollman said boastfully. "See if you can tie one like that!"

Phillips then pressed Hollman on his employment as a sailor.

Hollman testified he had worked as a third wheelman for the steamer The City of Milwaukee, which traveled from that location to his previous hometown of Grand Haven, Michigan.

One point of "doubt" for the jury had concerned Hollman's coat which had hung inside the Stuhmer farmhouse, which was said to have Fred Geddes shaving razor in a pocket. A "mystery man" emerged into the dialog earlier in witness testimony, and attorney Abraham Phillips knew the issue could also cause reasonable doubt.

Phillips reluctantly asked Hollman about the mystery man, who had departed employment at the farm soon after the discovery of the razor.

"Another man came in around noon," Hollman said, shortly after the moment he was hired. "He had on an overcoat like mine, only a little darker. I did not notice his cap."

Hollman explained he'd always hung his coat "on the west side of the kitchen" and that Louise Sthuhmer, wife of Hank, had moved it.

"I believe she took it out of that room and put it in the front room," Hollman said. He denied Louise Stuhmer ever telling him about the children finding a razor and if it belonged in "his pocket."

"I asked for my overcoat to go over to August Misch's place," Hollman said, regarding his brief departure from the Stuhmer farmhouse on the morning of December 6. "She took it out of the room (for me) and said nothing of a razor." Hollman also indicated his coat had a hole in a pocket due to rats chewing at it.

Prosecutor Phillips pointed out hours before his arrest Hollman had shreaded some of his garments and tried to dispose of them. Hollman explained that he tore up the clothing not to destroy evidence but because they were old and worn out.

He had placed the garments in the trash, and they were carried out to be disposed.

Hollman explained that his "swollen eyes" at the time of his arrest was due to a toothache.

Prosecutor Phillips then pointed to a map prepared for courtroom display. It featured the locations of all residences, farmland and roadways around the Geddes home. He questioned Hollman about the hedge again, the one which he claimed to have passed through on the Miner property along the road.

Q: How far is the road south of Miner's house?

A: About four or five rods (12-15 yards) from the fence. I went 15-20 rods (45 to 60 yards) from the gate and crawled through the hedge."

Prosecutor Phillips pointed out no hedge existed there. However, a very high hedge was farther down the road that was impassible, as a previous witness had testified.

Hollman again stated that in the early morning of December 6 when he departed the Stuhmer farmhouse, he did not reach the residence of August Misch and returned quickly only because it had rained and the road was slippery.

Phillips told the jury it was at this time the prosecution believed he had hidden the gold watch and the shaving razor.

Prosecutor Phillips noted it had not rained on Saturday, December 5, as Hollman and the men had worked all day in the field husking corn. And if there was rain, it occurred overnight.

"It was kind of slippery in the road, anyhow," Hollman explained. "There were some spots down the road, and my overshoes were pretty worn, and the ground stuck to them as I walked."

Hollman's testimony ended.

He returned to the seat beside Columbus Schneider at the defense table.

The defense watched as a few rebuttal witnesses were placed on the stand.

The prosecution and defense began their final arguments into early the evening. Proceedings ran late for the day, so court was dismissed.

Completion of closing statements would resume in the morning, then the case would then be handed over to the jury for decision.

PART 6

Sentenced to Death

Resumption of closing statements began the morning of Friday, April 16 around 9:00 and ended before noon. At 1:45, the case was given to the jury for decision. Hollman was escorted out of the courtroom and placed under guard in a private room. After organizing their materials, the jury broke for lunch.

They would deliberate the case after eating.

Hollman waited quietly inside the enclosed area outside the courtroom, seemingly confident he would be set free.

"The prisoner was in the dock, awaiting him life or death, with less apparent concern than any other person in the courtroom," one newspaper reported. "And his demeanor during the whole trial was in keeping with his appearance on the occasion."

The jury reassembled a little before 2:00 in the afternoon. The 12 men had reached a unanimous decision after deliberating for no more than 30 minutes.

The jury returned with a verdict at 2:45.

Hollman was returned to the courtroom with his attorney at his side.

It was reported that approximately 100 persons had jammed the courtroom during reading of verdict. Judge Sample read the decision aloud. The jury convicted Frederick Hollman of murder in the first degree and recommended he receive the death penalty by hanging.

Hollman turned pale upon hearing the verdict and faced the judge declaring that "a great wrong had been committed," and that the jury had "convicted an innocent man."

Concerned for his safety, Hollman also asked that the angry crowd be kept back.

Reviewing the jury's findings, the Judge discovered the jury had also concluded Hollman to be the killer of the other murdered women who were mentioned at trial. However, no further charges would be filed. Hollman was escorted back to the Ford County jail to await sentencing.

On April 21, Frederick Hollman was brought back before Judge Sample for sentencing. Hollman asked for a new trial. Sample informed him a motion had already been made by his defense attorney. Columbus Schneider wanted to retry the case asserting Hollman was not guilty by way of mental defect. The request for a new trial was denied.

Judge Alfred Sample then addressed Hollman as onlookers in the courtroom became silent.

"During my long years on the bar and 12 years on the bench," Sample stated, "I have never known a prisoner more ably defended, nor a jury more capable of giving a fair and impartial trial."

"The sentence of the court is pronounced on the verdict of the jury that the defendant, Frederick Hollman, alias Fred Hartman, be confined to the county jail until Friday, May 14, 1897. And on that day, between the rising and setting of the sun, at a place within the walls of the county jail at Ford County, or within an enclosure adjoining said jail, he be hanged by the neck until he is dead," Sample announced. "May God have mercy on his soul."

The moment Judge Sample completed addressing Hollman the convicted killer began to speak out.

"I don't want to be hanged," Hollman reportedly said in an outburst directed to Sample. "But, I must take things as they come. The jury hangs an innocent man. I have nothing to confess, except one thing, that I left my wife!"

He remained insistent that he was innocent of any crime.

Sheriff Benjamin Mason escorted Hollman back to the Ford County jailhouse to await execution.

Hollman was placed on "death watch" under the observance of Laurence Campbell, a 36-year-old stock dealer who lived in Gibson City with his wife and two sons. Sheriff Mason deputized Campbell for the assignment.

It appeared Frederick Hollman would die without a friend by his side. The Grand Haven Tribune reported his parents were deceased, and "his second wife (Gusta) hated him, as he hated her."

Julius Hallman, Frederick's brother who lived in Ripon, Wisconsin, had promised to help his him but never made an appearance at the jailhouse or at trial. Julius Hallman never contributed a cent to his brother's defense, either. No trace of him could be found. One report stated Julius Hollman had moved with his wife Maggie and children from Wisconsin to New York. Another speculated that Hallman still lived in Wisconsin in a neighboring county.

Hollman stated that he believed his wife Augusta knew nothing regarding his trial and sentence. "For that, I am thankful," he remarked.

"I am grateful she knows nothing of this, for it would be harder for me to bear if she and the children were here," Hollman said. He added that he had no desire to see her or their two children.

"If they stood at the door of this prison, I would not turn around to admit them."

Some jurors spoke to the press as they departed the courtroom and indicated that until the Hollman took the witness stand, they were leaning toward a life sentence, not execution.

A number of them said, "Hollman brought the death penalty upon himself."

Jurors also said Hollman's haggard appearance during the trial was "condemnatory."

Columbus Schneider confirmed the unanimous sentiment of the jurors. He told a reporter for The Pantagraph that during the trial it "became impossible to control the defendant."

Schneider confirmed that before Hollman testified "jurors were generally in favor of a life term as a penalty." He acknowledged when his client took the stand he knew that "the man's last chance was gone."

"His conduct on the (witness) stand and his contradictions and evasions led them (the jurors) unreservedly to a belief in his guilt and added to the impression of the enormity of his crime," Schneider stated. "When he (Hollman) retired from the witness stand the noose was firmly fixed on his neck. And, none of them regret the verdict they returned."

Schneider told the press a motion for a new trial was denied.

"Unless the Governor or Supreme Court shall intervene, Frederick Hollman, alias Fred Hartman, will pay with his life," attorney Schneider told the Paxton Record newspaper.

No sooner had Hollman been convicted of murder, Columbus Schneider wrote a letter to the Grand Haven Tribune, which was published in the April 24, 1897 edition. Essentially breaking with confidentiality between a client and representative counsel, Hollman's attorney spilled his guts regarding his non-paying client.

"I have certainly come into possession of facts which cause me to believe that he (Hollman) is the most cold blooded brute that ever breathed God's pure air," Schneider wrote in the letter published in the Grand Haven Tribune.

"He has not yet confessed to his crimes to me," Schneider wrote, "but I am convinced that he is guilty. I took this man's case hoping that I would be enabled to find his relatives and be remunerated for my time and expenses. Thus far, I have not found a man who will lend a helping hand."

During the trial, a massive amount of information and details concerning Frederick Hollman's exploits and his victims became available to the public for the first time. The shocking details became big news in the Gibson City Courier, Paxton Record and The Pantagraph in Bloomington.

It was not uncommon to see headlines and stories comparing Hollman to Jack the Ripper and H. H. Holmes.

H. H. Holmes had terrorized the Chicago area with his murderous ways and had been executed the previous year on May 7th. Since then, Holmes has become recognized as the first "serial killer" in America, in the modern sense of the term.

A story published in many newspapers around the nation days before Hollman's execution said the killer was "another H. H. Holmes." The headline of a May 14, 1897 article published in the Chicago Tribune stated Hollman's path of murder "Rivals The Holmes Case."

There was speculation that Holmes and Hollman might have even crossed paths at one time, but no evidence exists to substantiate it.

It was known Hollman frequently hung out on Clark Street while he was in Chicago, which was not much more than eight miles from the "Holmes Castle" in Englewood, Illinois.

On May 16, 1897, the New York Times published an article stating that Professor William Krohn and Doctors Wylie and Ragsdale of Gibson City, Illinois believed "the (Hollman) case is unique in criminology and psychology, like those of Jack the Ripper and H. H. Holmes."

"He (Hollman) equaled both in the number (of victims) and heartlessness of his crimes," the New York Times added. The article, comparing Hollman to Holmes, featured a headline that read, "A Jeckle and Hyde Executed."

There can be little doubt a man named Ned Conners, who lived no more than 12 miles from Paxton, was rattled by the press frequently comparing Frederick Hollman to H. H. Holmes.

Conners, a 40-year-old watchmaker, resided in Gibson City with second wife Anna.

Several years earlier, Conners had managed a first floor jewelry store in what had become known as Holmes Castle in the employment of Herman Webster Mudgett, a.k.a. H. H. Holmes. Conners lived with his first wife Julia and their daughter Pearl in a small apartment above the drug store.

Julia Conners was attracted to Mudgett and became pregnant by him. The Conners divorced over the matter and daughter Pearl was left in her mother's care.

Soon after the Conners' divorce, H. H. Holmes murdered Julia Conners on Christmas Day 1891, dissolved her organs and flesh with acid, and sold her skeleton to the Hahnemann Medical College for $200. Authorities found the skeletal remains of a young child, which was identified as Pearl.

Ned Conners remarried. He and second wife Anna moved from Chicago to Gibson City, where his second wife's family lived, in an effort to distance himself from the tragedies H. H. Holmes committed.

Frederick Hollman was not the only killer in 1897 to be compared to H. H. Holmes, however. One was a man named James Gordy.

On April 15, James M. Gordy of Milton, Delaware was convicted of murder in the killing his wife, Mary Estelle (Lewis) Gordy. He was hanged in Georgetown, Delaware on June 11.

Robert C. White, attorney general of Delaware compared Gordy to H. H. Holmes and told the press that his crimes "have been even more atrocious than those fastened upon the murderer Holmes."

But, unlike Hollman and Holmes, only one murder was attributed to Gordy.

Newspapers around the country published items about the Hollman and Gordy cases virtually at the same time. By coincidence, the April 19, 1897 front page of the Marietta Daily Leader, Ohio, announced hanging verdicts of both Hollman and Gordy only one news column apart.

After Frederick Hollman's trial, authorities from Wisconsin came to the Ford County jailhouse and "closely" interrogated him concerning the death of Bertha Hilgendorf.

The Pantagraph reported that "Schneider believes that Hollman murdered a woman in Wisconsin, for which crime her husband is now serving a life sentence in the penitentiary."

A small entourage of law officers from Wisconsin arrived at the Ford County jail and after aggressively questioning Hollman, stated "they were satisfied" that Hollman did not commit the murder of Bertha Hilgendorf.

Sheriff Benjamin Mason, who was present during questioning, issued a statement to the press that he agreed.

It is unknown if authorities or Columbus Schneider knew of information possessed by inmate William Kelly at the time. Apparently Hollman had confessed to being the true killer of Bertha Hilgendorf to Kelly during their incarceration, information that would not surface publicly until over a year and a half later.

It was not until two weeks after Hollman's sentencing that Columbus Schneider revealed how he had come to the conclusion of Hollman's guilt in the murder of Bertha Hilgendorf. Schneider said Hollman "had confessed to the killing" in secrecy and under the protection provided by lawyer/client privilege.

Schneider believed that once the death penalty had been carried out, the lawyer/client relationship was no longer valid.

Evidence suggested that Frederick Hollman was in Kenosha, five miles from the Hilgendorf residence, on July 4, 1896, attending Fourth of July festivities on the day of the murder. However, evidence also suggested at the time of the murder Hollman was employed cutting corn for a nearby farmer who lived only one mile from the Hilgendorf residence.

Hollman reportedly left town a day later but not before talking to neighbors near the scene and pointing the finger at August Hilgendorf, the dead woman's husband. Hollman had also provided details concerning how Bertha Hilgendorf had been murdered, which aroused suspicion, as some of the information was known only to police investigators, not the general public.

While Charles C. Howdyshell had been appointed to keep an eye on Hollman at the jailhouse, Deputy Laurence Campbell was assigned to keep a more attentive eye on the prisoner as his "suicide watch" guard.

Campbell, born in 1861 in Indiana, supplemented his income as stock dealer accepting work for Ford County in various capacities. During his brief time as deathwatch guard of Hollman the two stuck up a civil discourse, even a friendship, newspapers reported.

After tossing out several Lutheran pastors seeking to minister to him, Hollman made an exception allowing Reverend George Wilson access to his cell. Wilson, advanced in years, did not impose on Hollman to make any confession to any crimes attributed to him.

The two reportedly prayed together and a civil relationship developed, one which would continue until the day of Hollman's demise.

Wilson, age 79, was a Baptist Minister from McLean County's Bloomington Township. Initially, Wilson was the only minister whom Hollman permitted into his jail cell. Wilson became, according to the press, "Hollman's Spiritual Advisor."

George M. Wilson, born on August 22, 1817 in Allegheny County, Pennsylvania, lived most of his life in Bloomington Township with his wife and raising their seven children. Wilson was soft spoken, said to be a wealthy man, but lived humbly.

Wilson was ordained by the Mansfield Presbytery in 1841, the same year he married Margaret Taggart. After a few years he received immersion from the Baptist Church fostering an affiliation which remained. The Reverend was an author, as well. His published works included "Baptismal Controversy Reviewed," and "The Kingdom of God Developed: According to the Inspired Record and Predictions."

Wilson's wife passed away in 1887, the same year his second book was published.

After his wife's passing, Wilson was said to be a very lonely man. It is likely Wilson's loneliness and advanced age softened Hollman's abrasive demeanor.

George Wilson and Frederick Hollman shared interests. Both enjoyed the trade of farming and Wilson shared with Hollman his endeavors in the building up the industrial and agricultural interests in the community with his bare hands.

Wilson penned spiritual poetry as well, and read some of this to Hollman in his cell. It was said sentimental poetry "would bring tears" to Hollman's eyes.

One poem Wilson likely shared with Hollman Wilson concerned the loss of his wife, Margaret.

In part, it read:

Then I shall talk as spirits do, and learn
what now is known to you;

The life we now begin by faith, will not be
altered by death.

And when the Savior comes again, we hope
to follow in His train:

The earth a paradise will be, and here
again I'll walk with thee.

According to Reverend Wilson, Hollman spent a part of his time in jail marking specific passages in his Bible indicating a disposition to show his innocence.

"He (Hollman) says it will be a long time before the resurrection," Wilson remarked. "Evidently, he believes in some way he will reap an advantage from that fact."

According to reports, aside from Reverend Wilson, Laurence Campbell provided Hollman with some comfort, and was able to reason with him.

It was said that Campbell was one of the few people who could persuade the doomed man to temper his anger and behavior leading up to his hanging. Campbell often persuaded

Hollman to "bite his tongue" when it came to speaking against those who had convicted him, especially when the press wandered in taking notes near Hollman's cell.

Also in Hollman's company on a regular basis after his sentence was psychologist Professor Blome of the Rice Collegiate Institute. 43-year-old Blome served as a counselor to Hollman after his conviction and at times served as a spokesperson. Blome had acted as an assistant interpreter during Hollman's trail, as most of the testimony was spoken in German.

While awaiting execution, one visitor Hollman received was a former Grand Haven resident and acquaintance Charles Rosenbaum, age 29. Rosenbaum had been an employee of Charles Selighman, who owned a cigar store in Grand Haven where Hollman would hang out at times. Rosenbaum relocated and resided in Bloomington when he called on Hollman at the jailhouse.

An "interview" with Frederick Hollman made the pages of the May 3 edition of the Chicago Tribune. The newspaper said the reporter had spoken with Hollman on Wednesday, April 28. The Tribune reported that the writer had confronted Hollman about speaking the truth on the murder of Wiebke Geddes.

"Geddes got out all right," was all Hollman said of the matter. "I have nothing to say against Geddes."

The reporter told Hollman that if he would confess it could provide grounds for an effort to secure a reprieve or possibly a commuted sentence. In the reporter's words, it would prove he "was insane" when killing the women.

The reporter surmised that Hollman could "straighten out the matter" regarding August Hilgendorf, who was convicted for the murder of his wife Bertha, thereby possibly "restoring to liberty" the innocent party.

It was reported Hollman "thought about the matter," then became defiant with his response.

"I have nothing to straighten out," Hollman said to the reporter. "I am not a coward, that I cannot die like any other man. I want to die. I am glad my time is coming soon!"

The prisoner then made some disturbing threats.

"Just wait until I am dead and I will come back every night and visit those men who put me here, those witnesses and jurors," Hollman said. "I will haunt then to their graves. I will rap on their windows at night, and they will see my face at their windows. When I go to the scaffold I will make a speech. I will tell about them (the witnesses and jurors) and I will curse them. I will call down curses on their heads from heaven!"

When asked if he had any desire to see a clergyman of the Lutheran church, Hollman swore at the reporter and declared, "If a (Lutheran) preacher came inside my cell, I would knock his brains out!"

The Pantagraph newspaper reported Hollman said that he wished to be buried face down in the middle of the crossroads of town.

"Let those German around Melvin drive over me, if they dare," Hollman reportedly declared.

However, Hollman's temper and defiance softened during his final days. He even displayed sentimentality, thanks to the companionship of Laurence Campbell, Professor Blome, Sheriff Mason and in particular, the Reverend George Wilson.

Hollman displayed tears anytime conversations with Reverend Wilson included his mother, Augusta Leve. Both of Hollman's parents had been deceased for some time, but The Pantagraph reported, "when his mother is mentioned, he (Hollman) weeps like a child."

"The love he expressed for his first wife seemed to be the only human sentiment he entertained," Sheriff Mason told the press.

However, Hollman did not display any sentiment or remorse for any of his victims or their families. On that topic, he was said to "remain unmoved." Hollman's hatred of his second wife, Augusta, was equally defined, and never wavered.

Sheriff Mason told reporters that Hollman's deep hatred of Augusta was "likely the origin of his universal hatred for that sex (women)." Mason added Hollman contended women were "all bad, except that one," meaning his first wife Amelia.

As preparations for the impending hanging began taking place, Sheriff Mason had "tickets" printed that were mailed to or delivered to persons on May 6 as an invitation to the event. A list had been drafted that included area law enforcement officers, dignitaries, witnesses and jurors at the trial and family members and friends of Hollman's victims.

The ticket read:

Paxton, Illinois, May 6 1897.

Admit _____ to Jail on Friday, May 14th, 1897 to witness the execution of Fred Hoellmann, alias Fred Hartman.

B. F. Mason, Sheriff of Ford County.

Positively Not Transferable.

The name of the guest was handwritten on the line. Only persons bearing a ticket would have a chance to gain access to the jailhouse for the hanging. But, while 100 invitations were printed and delivered, only 50 persons would actually gain entry the morning of May 14.

Kevin Collier

One of the most unusual "final" requests granted for Frederick Hollman was the construction of a coffin with a glass window in the lid.

The request was believed to be due to the fact that in his native hometown of Brandenberg a custom-made casket was unheard of. Caskets in his native land were very simple in form and finish.

"This request was granted him," Professor William O. Krohn, a chairman of psychology at the University of Illinois, wrote in a published paper later on the subject. "A coffin with a glass in it—that others might have the privilege of looking on his face. Hollman thought himself greatly honored by being the only member of his father's family buried in a casket with a glass cover."

Sheriff Mason had promised Hollman the custom coffin as to grant a last wish. Construction of the coffin was completed on the evening of May 12. Hollman's request to see it was granted.

At 6 a.m. on May 12, after Hollman reported ate a "hearty breakfast," Sheriff Mason led Hollman down the steps from his second floor cell to the view the handsome rosewood coffin which would be placed beside the gallows. He carefully inspected with pride.

"He took great pleasure in finding the glass in the cover, and felt the satin lining with his fingers, expressing himself as greatly delighted thereat," Krohn wrote. "Not the slightest trace of fear or dread seemed to cross his mind."

Hollman rattled the handles on the coffin then turned to Sheriff Mason.

"You're all right, Sheriff," Hollman reportedly said. "You done what you agreed to. Let's go back."

Hollman then was returned to his cell.

The coffin was constructed by Ivis Luke Atwood, age 35, a furniture maker and proprietor of a local furniture business in Gibson City. Atwood was married to the former Susan Perdue and had a child, Jay P., who was nearly age one. Atwood charged $14 for the coffin, an equivalent of nearly $380 today.

The price also included a simple coroner's transport box.

The Paxton Record newspaper described the coffin as "neat," as in refined, skillfully done and tasteful in appearance. It is unlikely the entire coffin lid was made of glass. Descriptions mention "a pane" in a wooden lid in the area of the head, or a "window."

A glass viewing pane in the lid of a coffin corresponds with items displayed by the death museum near Oak Ridge Cemetery in Springfield, Illinois.

"I know they used to have coffins with a glass panel in them," Rosemary Kurtz, Paxton Carnegie Library Historian explained. "I saw them in a traveling museum."

When the scaffold was being constructed Hollman was said to maintain a "perfect nonchalance."

As the timbers were brought in, out of consideration for the prisoner, Sheriff Mason moved Hollman to a cell in a corridor where he would not be able to view the scene. Hollman protested and asked Mason if he could assist in the construction.

"I would rather help in the construction than be put off by myself," Hollman reportedly said. "Just sitting in a cell is so confining."

In charge of the construction of the gallows was John R. Moter of the nearby city of Danville, in Vermilion County. Moter had build the gallows for a much publicized double hanging on December 8, 1893 of murderers Harvey Pate and Frank Stires, who were executed for the robbery and murder of wealthy Pilot Township farmer Henry Helmick on August 25 that year.

The Hollman gallows was built in a room just off from the main floor corridor in a room that measured 34 by 19 feet. The mechanism was said to taken up one third of the room space.

The device was said to be of the strong construction and occupied a space about eight feet square. The main part of the structure was made of pine, while the top portion was made from oak. It was tested for 250 pounds, and was reported to have "worked without a hitch."

The hanging rope was three-eighths inch of linen cord. The trap door would be released by severing a cord positioned below with a knife.

The structure was said to have "worked with accuracy and precision." Passing inspection, the hanging platform was in wait.

The reports of Hollman assisting in the construction said the doomed man was "singing hymns and whistling" as he drove a nail in here, then there and then would stand back, with eyes gleaming, to admire his work.

Hollman seemed fascinated by the scaffold and even stood upon the trap door and looked upward examining the rope over his head.

"He (Hollman) was, by all accounts, a very obliging man who helped build his scaffold, hummed absently while it was tested with a sandbag, and stood patiently and politely," the Chicago Tribune reported in an article published on June 15, 1959, which recounted the spectacle during Ford County, Illinois' centennial celebration.

A local reporter, summoned when the scaffold was being erected, was allowed to speak with Hollman. While the reporter had difficulty understanding precisely what the condemned man said, he translated it best he could.

"I am innocent of the crime charged against me," Hollman told the reporter. "I have been locked up here five months, and it seems to me a year or more, and I am glad my time has arrived. Mr. Blome has sent me papers and books and everybody has treated me kindly. But, my friends went back on me."

Hollman reportedly gently kicked one of the sandbags attached to the hanging rope as he was returned to his cell.

On the morning of May 13, during a dress rehearsal one day before his execution, Frederick Hollman requested a photographer to take a picture of him posing on the gallows. Hollman was neatly attired in a black Prince Albert suit, and reportedly looked "little (not) like a murderer."

There was said to be a touch of sentiment to the request, so Sheriff Mason allowed it.

Gibson City photographer and artist Olaf Rasmus was summoned and arrived shortly before noon. Hollman was accompanied to the gallows by Sheriff Mason, Laurence Campbell and another guard, Vinton Flora.

Hollman struck a deal with Rasmus reaching an agreement that copies of the photograph would be sold to the public and half the proceeds devoted to procurement of a coffin and transport of his remains to Grand Haven, Michigan.

Hollman wished to be buried beside his first wife and two children in the plot he purchased in Lake Forest Cemetery in 1886.

The photographer promised that "this shall be done."

With Deputy Laurence Campbell and Sheriff Benjamin Mason at Hollman's sides, Rasmus began taking pictures as Hollman posed. He reportedly took several photos to ensure a "good one for commercial release."

In his hand, for the photographs, Hollman held his Bible. Some reports said the Bible came with him from Germany 13 years earlier, while other newspapers reported that the Bible was actually the one Sheriff Mason had given him when he was first lodged in the Ford County jail.

Hollman took great care to hold the holy book outward for the camera, as to display it.

"He was very proud of his Bible," Professor William O. Krohn wrote later in a report of the moment, based on interviews with those who were present at the event. "On it (the cover of the Bible) was inscribed 'As for me and my house, we will serve the

Lord.' This he carefully held toward the camera when his picture was taken on the scaffold."

"When his picture was taken on the death-trap of the gallows, he manifested the most marked vanity conceivable," Krohn wrote concerning Hollman's strange behavior. "From every particular about his pose, with chin pointed out and head up in the air, one would think he regarded himself in his self-centered, vain conceit as the envy of all men."

As he posed holding his Bible, Hollman called upon heaven to witness that he was "an innocent man" and that he "had never killed any woman."

According to an article published in 1956 recounting the event, Chicago Tribune columnist Thomas Morrow said that Hollman "conducted the first commercial" known from a scaffold.

"He let it be known that he would like to have his picture taken in his new hanging uniform with a couple of jailers by his side," Thomas Morrow wrote. "After the execution," Hollman was reported to have said, "you can sell the picture and defray the expense of my burial."

Historians note the selected photo did sell, but no money went to a proposed Hollman burial in Grand Haven. A "gallows" photograph was not published in any newspaper at the time, as the technology was scarce and cost to do so prohibitive.

It would be decades later when any of the photos would be published, and republished.

Later the afternoon of May 13, Hollman scribbled out a document requesting that the "income from the sale of his gallows" be given to the men (Charles C. Howdyshell and Laurence Campbell) who "have acted as my death watch."

He also asked for the sale of his execution garments to also help assist with costs to transport his body to Grand Haven, as well as the sale of parts of the gallows.

This statement dumbfounded those who heard it, as Hollman had no authority concerning the sale of his garments or gallows, which were the property of Ford County.

Hollman also rehearsed his final speech on May 13, which he would not read himself the morning of his execution.

The most widely known photo of infamous "gallows portrait" was published in 1959 as part of a commemorative Ford County Centennial Edition. In the picture, the manacle of a pair of handcuffs is visible on Hollman's wrist. Sheriff Mason had uncuffed the other manacle for Hollman to be able to display his Bible. Hollman held the loose manacle in that hand, which he placed on his hip, turned away from the camera.

"He (Hollman), himself, looked like a pastor of some church, in his long, black frock coat and a white tie," a newspaper reported on May 14, 1897, concerning the garments Hollman wore in the photographs.

Ironically, that was how Hollman was identified in the 1959 Ford County Centennial Edition. A man noted as a "minister" in the cutline beneath the photo is, in fact, Hollman.

The cutline correctly identifies Sheriff Benjamin Mason at left, but notes the man in the middle as only "deputy." Historians have speculated that man is either Ira Gilmore or Laurence Campbell, however, it is Campbell. The real "minister" in the room that morning, George Wilson, Hollman's spiritual advisor, was not in the photograph.

Photo of Hollman on the Gallows by Olaf Rasmus

In the days leading up to Hollman's execution, large crowds gathered outside of the Ford County jailhouse. There was said to be a "suppressed excitement" in the air. Hundreds of citizens applied for admission and entered the jailhouse in a procession to see the gallows that had been constructed.

Gatherers, mostly citizens of Ford County and Drummer Township, talked amongst themselves about the crimes and impending final punishment of the convicted man. Little doubt was expressed by the crowd as to Hollman's guilt, and little sympathy was forthcoming.

It was to be the first execution in Ford County. Historically, it would the only execution ever conducted in the county. Newspapers enjoyed increased sales as readers hungered for any details of the killer, his crimes, or the scheduled execution.

Frederick Hollman claimed he had never granted "an interview" with a reporter, "although alleged interviews have been sent out," The Pantagraph explained. Hollman did speak broken English, but most the quotes attributed to him were translated from German to English either by his handlers or reporters. The Pantagraph theorized other newspapers were making up material said to have been the result of interviews.

However, many quotes reporters published from Hollman resulted from them hanging in the hall eavesdropping near his jail cell as he spoke to a guard or visitor. An actual sit down or one-on-one "interview" likely occurred only twice during Hollman's incarceration.

It was reportedly on May 12 as many as 500 visitors who had come to view the gallows and just as many had appeared on May 13, the day before the execution.

Just when it seemed the story of a killer was all but over, a witness and victim of Hollman showed up at the Ford County jailhouse the day before his execution.

A woman named Mary Elizabeth Schertz came forward with information that Frederick Hollman had tried to kill her during an attack and "had confessed" at that moment to being a "multi-murder."

Schertz, 31-years-old, told authorities of an attack that happened to her in McLean County the fall of 1896, taking place before the murders of Carrie Lenz and Wiebke Geddes.

According to Schertz, during the attack Hollman had said while clutching her throat, "I have killed other women and I will kill you!" Schertz' brother Peter witnessed the attack and had rescued her from her assailant. The unidentified man had fled on foot.

Schertz made a positive identification of Hollman as he said in his jail cell. Hollman reportedly became enraged and "threatened to kill" Schertz during the brief visit. Sheriff Mason calmed the situation and her statement of the assault was taken.

Hollman's attorney Columbus Schneider issued a statement to The Pantagraph that he believed his client would fess up to his crimes before the final curtain fell.

"I am confident Hollman will make a statement which will amount to a confession, either tonight or from the gallows tomorrow," Schneider said.

The general public was unsure of the precise time Hollman would be hanged, as Sheriff Mason declined to give out the hour of execution.

The limited number of people who received tickets to the event were given a time of 6:00 a.m. to be at the jailhouse, thus the press assumed the hanging itself would take place no later than an hour after that time.

A large crowd outside the jailhouse was expected early on the morning of May 14. Newspapers reported farmers from the town of Melvin, where Wiebke Geddes was murdered, were arriving by train. The Pantagraph reported, "They (the citizens of Melvin) are determined to see Hollman die, even if they have to break into the jail."

Sheriff Mason expressed little concern over the threat, but relayed to the press that he would be "taking no chances."

Frederick Hollman had spent the last the last five months jailed in a cell on the second level of the Ford County jailhouse. On the afternoon of May 13 Frederick Hollman was transferred to a cell on the east side of the main floor. The gallows stood only 20 feet away, which was clearly in his view.

A visitor was allowed inside the main corridor every few minutes to view the scaffold. Hollman would come to the bars of his cell to get a look at the newcomer, and ask Deputy Campbell or guard Houdshell who he or she was.

Then Hollman glanced at the gallows with a critical eye.

Psychology students from Professor Rudolph Blome's class from Rice Institute had visited Hollman in his cell that afternoon. Blome and the class of students sang a number of hymns for his benefit. It was said there were "few dry eyes" in the corridor at that moment.

However, it was reported that Hollman's "mental and physical makeup" was "a puzzle to the students of psychology" whom had paid Hollman a visit.

Hollman's overall appearance had improved greatly after his trial, but degraded rapidly that afternoon. Previously he had been shaven, his hair neatly trimmed and "looked like any other common man," one newspaper reported.

But after mid-day, May 13, that all changed.

"He looked badly," one newspaper observed, adding Hollman had "failed rapidly since noon."

Hollman's face appeared flush and his demeanor nervous.

It was reported near the end Hollman would be sobbing with grief and protest his innocence one moment, and the next would be cracking jokes, playing tricks and making fun, as though no serious threat was before him.

Early that evening, Frederick Hollman was visited by a German Lutheran minister who arrived to administer the last sacrament, but the meeting went awry. The minister explained he could not perform the last sacrament until the killer confessed.

"Then you can get right out of here," Hollman told the minister, and threw him out. Hollman would make no admission as to his guilt.

Before the Ford County jail closed to the public at 9:30 that evening, a reporter from The Pantagraph arrived. Hollman was singing hymns in his cell with Professor Blome, Reverend Wilson and Deputy Laurence Campbell at the time. Hollman briefly spoke to the reporter and Professor Blome helped translate the broken English. What Hollman conveyed was an eerie sense of resolve about his impending fate.

"Well, I shan't be singing tomorrow night," Hollman said. "I am ready to go and forgive the people who are taking my life. I am innocent of the charge against me, but that makes no difference now. I have been with women and they have acted bad to me. Mr. Blome will make my statement tomorrow when I go out to die. I have made no talk to anyone about this except to Mr. Blome. He is a good man, so is Mr. Wilson. I shall sleep little tonight."

According to Sheriff Mason, shortly after the jail closed at 9:30 p.m., Hollman slept for "about two hours." Mason had told The Pantagraph earlier that day that he "did not relish" his impeding job as executioner, but would do his job "quietly."

Around 11 p.m., Reverend Eric Peter Ollson arrived at the jail and was allowed access to Hollman in his cell. About that time, Sheriff Mason departed and retired to his home at the jailhouse.

While Hollman was denied last sacrament by all of the ministers from the German Lutheran churches, he was granted it by Reverend Ollson, who was from the Swedish Lutheran Church of Paxton. Ollson had been pastor of the congregation for 9 years at the time.

Reverend Ollson, age 39, lived in Paxton with his wife Esther and 3-year-old son, Pherstanburg. Ollson had suffered the loss of an eight-month-old daughter just 3 months earlier.

Reverend Ollson shared communion with Hollman along with Professor Blome and Reverend Wilson.

It was generally said that Frederick Hollman had surrendered his defiant attitude and had become more penitent within the last week. Some reports claimed that Hollman returned steadfastly to his faith for comfort.

Reverend Ollson and Reverend Wilson placed no conditions on administering the final sacrament to Hollman. The two ministers of faith reasoned that Hollman's secret lay "between himself and his God," and "it was not for a man to interfere" unless the Higher Power "should move the criminal to open his heart."

The four men read scripture and sang hymns together. After a time, Reverend Ollson departed the cell and Hollman expressed his appreciation to the fellow Lutheran.

Wilson, Blome and Campbell remained with Hollman for the entire night and Charles Howdyshell remained seated just outside Hollman's cell for the duration.

Hollman reportedly talked freely with Wilson that night and professed his "conversion to his faith in the forgiveness of his own sins." But Hollman never confessed as to what those "sins" might include.

Reverend Wilson had informed the press earlier that day that Hollman "might confess to his crimes" the moment before his execution, but it would be only "of his own notion."

"He would not (confess) under persuasion," Wilson said. "Hollman appears to have got fixed on one idea, that he was not proven guilty, and he constantly reiterates that statement."

Sounds of prayer and hymns being sung were heard throughout the night until sunrise when Hollman was escorted to the scaffold and would hang for his crimes.

It was reported that a great deal of pressure was brought to bear on Illinois Governor John Riley Tanner to pardon Hollman the in the 24 hours leading up to his execution.

But a reprieve never came.

Kevin Collier

PART 7

Frederick Hollman's Execution

It was cold and overcast at dawn on May 14, 1897. A light, misty rain fell as Frederick Hollman reportedly glanced out of a tiny window in the rear of his cell. An onlooker said he did this "for a time."

Everything looked "somber and gloomy" that morning, one newspaper reported.

Hollman, who had not slept the night, returned to his religious meditations while staff prepared his breakfast. He prayed with Professor Blome and Reverend Wilson and the three men sang hymns.

Hollman was served breakfast at 6:00. He said he was "not hungry," and did not consume a single bite.

He dressed in his formal garments, described as a "black Prince Albert suit," which he had worn for the photographs taken on gallows the previous day.

Outside the jailhouse a crowd had been gathering overnight. Many curious out-of-towners came to Paxton by train early that morning.

"Possibly 1,000 people" had arrived in town for the event, it was reported.

The numbers were astounding, as the entire city of Paxton had a population of only 2,300 residents.

100 tickets had been printed and sent out to select individuals to gain admission into the jailhouse to view the hanging, but no more than 50 were allowed entrance due to space.

At 6:30, spectators were allowed inside. Upon entering, they heard Hollman in his cell, accompanied by Blome and Wilson, engaged in prayer and singing "Nearer My God, to Thee."

Once the allotment filled the cramped corridor, which led to the death chamber, the doors were closed behind them. Sheriff Mason asked all to remove their hats. The men smoked and chattered softly about the events of the previous days leading to this solemn moment.

It was reported that Frederick Hollman grew nervous as he heard the spectators entering.

Among the public for the viewing was Fred Geddes, husband of Wiebke Geddes. Also in attendance was Albert Lenz, husband of Carrie Lenz, and the woman's father, Matthias Bauman.

Present that morning for Frederick Hollman's execution were two sheriffs from neighboring cities; James Sloan, age 42, was the Sheriff of city of Danville, located a few miles south-west of Gibson City and Charles Edwin Johnston, age 45, the Sheriff of the city Peoria.

Hollman had been lodged at Sloan's jailhouse in Danville under his custody from the end of December 1896 until early January 1897 when Sheriff Benjamin Mason moved the prisoner after he uncovered a plot by Drummer Township citizens to break into the Ford County jailhouse to apprehend and lynch the killer.

Sheriff Johnston attended the execution that morning in an official capacity.

Johnston, who had been elected to the office of Sheriff in Peoria 1894, had experience as executioner. Johnston's jailhouse in Peoria had a permanent gallows, which was disassembled and moved to Tazewell County for the purpose of hanging convicted murderer Albert Wallace on March 14, 1896. Johnston reportedly had "pulled the drop" on the gallows ending Wallace's life.

At 6:50, accompanied by Professor Rudolph Blome, Hollman departed his cell and was escorted to the gallows.

Hollman stood silent before the scaffold he had helped to build.

One newspaper reported the wooden structure "stood like a sentinel of death."

Jail officials carried a board with them to strap Hollman to in the event that he would break down at the last moment and collapse before the hanging.

At Hollman's side were his jail guard Charles Houdyshell and spiritual advisor, Reverend George Wilson. Wilson and Blome urged Hollman to be steadfast. Both feared that there might be an incident if he was aroused. The two men appealed to Hollman's sentiment by starting up a hymn.

Singing hymns at his execution were Paxton Mayor John P. Middlecoff, city bookkeeper William C. Crary and Justice of the peace Jacob W. Preston. Hollman joined in.

Hollman's quavering voice in song occasionally reportedly rose above the others.

In his hands the doomed man held his Bible.

After the opening hymn, there was a moment of silence. Then the gathering sang "Jesus, Lover of My Soul," written by Charles Wesley in 1740.

Jesus, lover of my soul,
let me to Thy bosom fly.
While the nearer waters roll,
while the tempest still is high!
Hide me, O my Savior, hide—
till the storm of life is past;
safe into the haven guide,
O receive my soul at last!

Other refuge have I none—
hangs my helpless soul on Thee.
Leave, ah, leave me not alone;
still support and comfort me!
All my trust on Thee is stayed—
All my help from Thee I bring.
Cover my defenseless head
with the shadow of Thy wing.

Plenteous grace with Thee is found,
grace to cover all my sin;
let the healing streams abound;
make and keep me pure within.

Thou of life the fountain art—
Freely let me take of Thee;
spring Thou up within my heart;
rise to all eternity.

The song was followed by Frederick Hollman singing a German hymn that he had learned in the little village of Leonars, Brandenburg as a child. The hymn was "Let Me Go, So That I May See Jesus."

This proved too much for Hollman's self-control.

At the song's conclusion, Hollman reportedly broke into "violent sobs." After being calmed by Laurence Campbell, Professor Blome and Reverend Wilson, Hollman asked for a cup of water, but took only a few sips.

The corridor then became silent at the Sheriff Mason's command when at 7:09 he read the death warrant aloud for all to hear. Then Professor Blome stepped to the front of the platform.

Hollman hitched his shoulders and moved his feet uneasily.

"I have been asked to read the dying man's last statement," Blome began. "Here it is."

Frederick Hollman's final statement read:

I must die and find my deathbed in this way. I hold no malice toward any one. I freely forgive, as I ask God for Christ's sake to forgive me. Think not that I must close my lips because another speaks for me.

I am not guilty of the crime for which I die. I leave it all with God, who, in the judgment day, will give each the reward of his deeds. I believe that one who does not confess to God his sins is eternally lost. I have confessed to God and trust in him.

The rich, instead of spending their money for theater and the opera, should build hospitals and almshouses for the poor. Some day those who spend their money in this way may find themselves in the condition of the rich man who despised Lazarus.

I am glad that I am so near the end. I ask that my body be sent to Grand Haven, Michigan, and placed beside that of my wife and child.

Through the efforts of Reverend G.H. Wilson I have been saved. He has been with me during the last night of my life. I thank him now for his kindness.

Signed, Fred Hollman.

Hollman stood erect and looked straight ahead during the reading, but broke down and cried aloud when line "Some day those who spend their money in this way may find themselves in the condition of the rich man who despised Lazarus" was read.

Laurence Campbell patted him on the shoulder, an act of kindness that "completely restored his wavering courage," one report said.

Unknown to virtually everyone present, Frederick Hollman's final statement originally contained two lines that were deleted.

It was reported the two sentences showed "bitter rancor" toward "those ministers" who had first called on Hollman in his jail cell. "Those" were the ministers who had refused to administer the holy sacrament to him. Hollman had kicked them out of his cell and threatened violence upon them.

It was reported Hollman allowed those two sentences to be omitted at the strong suggestion of Reverend Wilson.

Frederick Hollman was then escorted up the steps to the hanging platform while a quartet of male voices began to sing "Nearer My God, to Thee," which Hollman had sung in his cell an hour earlier with Professor Blome and Reverend Wilson.

The words of "Nearer, My God to Thee," a hymn written by Sarah Flower Adams, loosely based on Genesis 28: 11-12, was said to have echoed throughout the corridors. According to some accounts, the hymns sung that morning were heard by the crowd gathered outdoors through the bars of the window openings of the jailhouse.

Sheriff Johnston bound Hollman's wrists, arms, knees and ankles with straps.

Hollman assisted him by bringing his limbs together.

Johnston placed the black death cap on Frederick Hollman's head and adjusted the noose around the doomed man's neck.

"Goodbye, Fred," the Reverend Wilson and Professor Blome both spoke to Frederick Hollman.

"Yes, goodbye," Hollman replied. "Goodbye everybody; goodbye everybody. Remember me."

What happened next is uncertain as two versions entered newspaper accounts.

According to one report, Hollman was about to say something but was cut off by Laurence Campbell and Sheriff Mason.

The other report said Hollman began "blasting into an accusatory rage" of condemnation.

The Pantagraph of Bloomington reported that after Hollman said, "Goodbye! Goodbye! Goodbye, *all of you, you will...*"

Laurence Campbell, who was on the platform, tapped Hollman on the shoulder as to interrupt him.

Hollman reported said one more "Goodbye," as his final word.

The Pantagraph also reported that just before Johnston adjusted the black cap upon his head, Hollman asked Sheriff Mason for permission to say a word. Mason replied, "No Fred. Don't talk anymore. It will be over in a minute."

Hollman accepted the Sheriff's reply without objection.

However, according to the Gibson City Courier, Hollman's voice rose and his vindictiveness asserted itself.

"Goodbye, you men who have killed me," the Gibson City Courier reported Hollman said, in a frenzy. "Goodbye, there will be justice. I will see you in hell."

It was believed by those in Frederick Hollman's company at the execution that the condemned man intended to renew threats against the jurors who convicted him and Lutheran ministers who refused him communion.

Hollman had stated to a Chicago Tribune reporter on April 28, "When I go to the scaffold I will make a speech. I will tell about them (the witnesses and jurors) and I will curse them. I will call down curses on their heads from heaven!"

This published threat was fresh on the minds of persons in authority there at the execution.

It was also reported Hollman once threatened his own defense attorney, Columbus Schneider.

Sheriff Mason and the others believed Hollman "intended to reiterate remarks of this kind previously made," when they urged his silence.

Whether or not Hollman said "I will see you in hell" moments before his hanging, Gibson City Courier reported it, and many other newspapers picked up the article and reprinted it.

As Hollman was about to utter a cry, Sheriff Mason swung the hatchet held in his hand at 7:17 a.m. to cut the rope attached to the trap doors beneath the doomed man's feet. Hollman shot down and hung in place at seven feet. The fall broke his neck.

There was not a quiver to his muscles, nor did Hollman move or turn. Spectators stood awestruck, silent and perfectly still.

Fred Geddes was reported to "look on with a quiet, thoughtful face." Albert Lenz and Matthias Bauman were said to display "expressions of satisfaction."

In 13 minutes his pulse waned. By 18 minutes his heart stopped beating. After 19 minutes his body was cut down. Hollman had died without a struggle.

Doctors Samuel Mack Wylie of Paxton and John E. Ragsdale of Gibson City, who were situated below the gallows trap, pronounced Hollman dead. His body was placed in the glass lid coffin situated beside the gallows.

Ragsdale believed that Hollman "was practically dead from fright when the trap fell."

Spectators in attendance were asked to leave. Hollman's remains would lay in his coffin in that room the until late afternoon.

Doctors Wylie and Ragsdale discovered Hollman's neck to have been broken just below the base of the brain, which explained his lack of motion during the execution.

The dead man's features were calm and composed, with the exception of slight discoloration around his neck where the rope had been.

Reverend George Wilson retired at the rear of the corridor minutes after the hanging and sat with his face in his outstretched hands. Reporters approached Wilson eager to discover whether Hollman had made a confession to any of the murders before his demise.

"No," Wilson said to one writer. "There is not a word to add to the statement made by Professor Blome on the gallows. The man died penitent, but he did not confess that he was guilty of the crime of murder."

It was reported that "no one in Paxton" believed a mistake had been made when Hollman was executed. There was no doubt in their minds of his guilt in the murder of Wiebke Geddes and the presumption of his guilt concerning the other murders attributed to him.

Hollman, the man the Gibson City Courier said "is one of the most extraordinary criminals of the age, ranking with Jack the Ripper" was dead.

Left behind in Frederick Hollman's jail cell was a sheet of paper, upon which was a poem he had been writing.

The poem was titled "Legendary." It read:

My name is Frederick Hoellmann,
I come from a far off country,
Which follows the river Rhine,
To America I journeyed
In honest to toll,
And now they gonna hang me,
And raise a great turmoil.
On 14 day of May,
When flowers are in bloom,
Between sunrise and sunset,
I must meet my fatal doom.
They said I did a murder,
but that I will deny....

The poem left off at those words, and was never completed. If not legendary, the final words attributed to Hollman were an echo of his "fatal doom."

But much like Hollman's unfinished poem, the story of Hollman's great acts of turmoil was far from complete. The toll from his deeds would endure and leave much unresolved.

Outside of the jailhouse in the rain and cold, the crowd "talked in their own language," as one newspaper reported. They displayed little excitement or emotion.

Most of the gathering dispersed by 8:00 that morning and only a few remained.

The press caught Fred Geddes and Albert Lenz as they departed the Ford County jailhouse and briefly interviewed both.

John Stroth, owner of the farmland and residence where Mrs. Geddes was murdered, served as interpreter for Fred Geddes.

"I am glad Hollman is dead," Geddes said. "It does not bring back my wife, but it will save others. She was a good wife, but she is gone."

Geddes was then asked about his six-year-old daughter Elizabeth's welfare, to which he responded, "The little girl is doing well."

Albert Lenz stated that Hollman was only 90 rods (a little over a quarter mile) from their home in Danforth when his wife was murdered and that the killer had only been absent from the place he was staying that night.

"I am certain that Hollman killed my wife," Albert Lenz said to the reporter.

Lenz also noted that a man seen trying to break into another German home on November 26 less than a mile away before his wife's murder. Lenz recalled the perpetrator gave up when he couldn't gain entry into the locked residence.

"We now believe up there that it was Hollman," Lenz said. "Suppose he had got in and killed the woman? When her husband returned and found her dead he would have been suspect in the murder, wouldn't he?"

Neighbors at the time thought the man attempting a break-in was a traveling tramp.

"It is awful to have such beasts as Hollman in the world," Lenz added.

Some gathered that day carried away unusual souvenirs.

According to the Paxton Record, the rope used to hang Hollman was "cut into small bits and given to those who desire as a relic of the occasion."

The gallows was dismantled and some of the scrap lumber found its way into the hands of children as souvenirs.

One Gibson City boy named Arthur Sandberg, who owned a piece of the wood, would recall later in life how his parents, once knowing where it had come from, would not permit the "treasure" to be brought into the house.

It was written the feeling in the town seemed to be "one of lost innocence," and that the purity and goodness had been violated, all because of one man, Frederick Hollman.

Kevin Collier

PART 8

The Plight of Hollman's Remains

Professor Blome, the man who read Frederick Hollman's last statement, was committed to seeing to it his final request to be buried beside his wife and children in Lake Forest Cemetery in Grand Haven, Michigan achieved.

Born Rudolph Harin Heinrich Blome in 1854 in Hoyerhagen, Hannover, Germany, Blome emigrated with his family to the United States at the age of fourteen.

After completing high school in Illinois, Blome decided to pursue a career in teaching and received a teacher's certificate from Northwestern College at Naperville in 1877. He taught in several elementary schools before securing a position in 1883 as the Principal of Schools in Elmhurst, Illinois, the same year Frederick Hollman immigrated to America.

In 1890, Blome graduated from Illinois State Normal School. From 1892 to 1897 he served as principal of Rice Collegiate Institute at Paxton.

Blome and his wife, Mary Jane (Pierce), had four children.

It was during Blome's service at Rice Collegiate Institute that he was called upon to counsel Frederick Hollman at the Ford County jailhouse.

Blome wrote a letter regarding the condemned man's final wish and telegraphed it to Grad Haven.

Blome's Telegram to Grand Haven

Professor Rudolph H. H. Blome's telegram was received by Charlie Hallman in Grand Haven, Michigan, moments after his cousin's execution.

The message concerned Frederick Hollman's burial request and delivery of his remains. It read:

My Dear Bro.—

Fred Hollman, who was executed here this morning asked to be buried at Grand Haven beside his wife. I was with him in his last moments and I promised him that I would see what could be done. In order that I may keep my pledge with the dying man I ask you to tell me whether his body will be received if sent free of all charges to Grand Haven. If there be any charges to bury him please tell me what they are.

You may have had this request before from some other source. I write to satisfy my own conscience. You are not asked to receive him if you do not wish to. I am not urging the matter, but would be pleased to have you write me the decision in the matter.

Should he be received we can send you the number of his lot in the cemetery though I have it not at hand this moment. If you will receive him please telegraph 'yes' at my expense. We are not trying to get rid of him, only to gratify his wishes.

Yours in Christ,

R.H.H. Blome

The Grand Haven Tribune published Blome's letter and reported that Hollman's body would be brought to Grand Haven for proper burial.

"That seems to be a settled fact," the newspaper said.

In 1886, Frederick Hollman had purchased a plot at Lake Forest cemetery. It was the location where first wife Amelia, their daughter Minnie and a stillborn child were buried.

"It was his dying request that he be buried beside them," the Tribune said. "There will be objection and it seems no more than humane, brute though he was, that his last wish be gratified. Those who interested themselves in his (Hollman's) behalf in Paxton will undoubtedly pay the necessary expenses, and the remains can be expected next Monday afternoon or Tuesday morning."

The intention was to have the body delivered to Charlie Hallman who would see to the burial. It is likely these arrangements were discussed via telegraph from Ford County to Grand Haven days before Hollman's execution.

It is known Charlie Hallman was in communication with both Blome and attorney Columbus Schneider concerning the remains.

During the Friday afternoon of May 14, word surfaced that Frederick Hollman's final request would not be granted. Information was made public that Charlie Hallman "will not be receiving the body if shipped there."

Attorney Schneider quickly issued a statement saying Charlie Hallman had written to him (via telegram) and refused receipt of the body.

"He wrote he'd ship it back if it came," Schneider told the press.

Charlie and his wife had no doubt become the center of attention in Grand Haven due to the execution and the plight of Hollman's remains. The general population of Grand Haven gossiped quite a bit about the affair.

Adding insult to injury, the Chicago Tribune made sport of Hollman's final "Grand Haven" request by quoting part of his final statement where the city was mentioned.

"Well, suppose you had a body to send," a Chicago Tribune columnist wrote. "Could you think of a better place (than Grand Haven)?"

There is little evidence that contact was attempted or made with other next-of-kin as an alternative location to ship Hollman's remains.

Usually in an execution, the condemned man directed who should be contacted regarding their remains.

It is possible Augusta Hollman was notified upon the death of her husband, but if so, it was likely Ford County officials did so in regards to a certificate of death.

It is unlikely that Augusta Hollman was asked if she wanted to claim the body. She did not want him back after he had abandoned her and there is no evidence to believe that sentiment had changed.

The afternoon and evening editions of the May 14 Illinois newspapers had reported that two physicians were "confident" that they will "get possession of the remains in the interest of science."

Late that afternoon, Judge Sample issued a temporary order in accordance with the Illinois state statute that "should no relative appear to claim the body" that Hollman's remains be turned over to Doctors Wylie and Ragsdale for post mortem examination.

The two men, Doctor Samuel Mack Wylie, age 42, of Paxton and Doctor John E. Ragsdale, age 45, of Gibson City, also served as coroners for Ford County.

What was described as a "simple wooden casket" was brought in to the Ford County jailhouse and Hollman's body was removed from his custom rosewood coffin and placed inside of it for transport to the coroner's office.

Casket builder Ivis Atwood, Doctor Frank B. Lovell, area funeral home owner Wallace S. Lamb and Lycurgus Burns helped place Hollman's remains into the six-foot long box constructed with a hasp.

When the body was removed from the jail, a lingering crowd outside followed the casket as it was loaded into a carriage and taken to the undertaker's.

That evening, Wylie and Ragsdale were joined by Professor William O. Krohn, a chairman of psychology at the University of Illinois. Krohn would oversee the autopsy of the body and examination of Hollman's brain.

The May 17, 1897 edition of the Grand Haven Tribune reported that Hollman's remains would not be returning to Grand Haven and published the gruesome details.

"The remains of Hollman, arch murderer and degenerate will not be buried in Lake Forest cemetery," the Tribune reported. "Word received from Paxton, Illinois, today was to the effect that his remains had already been disposed of, it is believed by medical and scientific men."

According to the Paxton Record, Hollman's body was buried in Glen Cemetery, in Paxton.

"It was placed in a neat coffin and buried in the potter's field (area) in that place," the newspaper reported. Doctor John E. Ragsdale of Gibson City confirmed he oversaw the burial at this place with a small accompaniment with a private graveside service conducted by Reverend George Wilson.

The burial casket was the one Hollman had requested from Sheriff Mason. While Hollman's body had been transported from the Ford County jailhouse in a simple wooden box for post-ortum examination at the office of the coroner, he was buried in the rosewood, satin-lined coffin with a glass pane in the lid.

No headstone was placed to mark its exact location of Hollman's remains.

An unauthenticated photo claiming to show Hollman's grave site was published 40 years after his death. In the picture a small stature, weathered, white picket fence outlined a location said to be the location Hollman's burial.

There were reports that Frederick Hollman's body was used as a cadaver by medical students in the Chicago area then "disposed of." If students did study the body, it was briefly after the official autopsy, then it was returned to Paxton. Hollman's remains were not "disposed of," but were, in fact, buried in Glen Cemetery.

Ironically, "others" did not "have the privilege" of looking upon Hollman's face through the glass pane in the coffin lid as he had imagined.

While his body was laid to rest, Frederick Hollman was buried without his head.

Kevin Collier

Before burial, Frederick Hollman's body had come into the possession of Professor William O. Krohn, a chairman of psychology at the University of Illinois and Doctor Samuel Wylie and Doctor John Ragsdale.

Professor William O. Krohn, who oversaw the examination, was 29-years-old at the time. He had just founded a laboratory for the study of the mentally ill at Eastern Hospital for the Insane in Kankakee, Illinois.

Hollman's brain was removed from his skull and was examined. Subsequent examinations of the brain would take place for over a year and a half as a broader psychological report was prepared.

The initial report issued to the press days after his death indicated Hollman possessed an abnormality akin to a Dr. Jeckle and Mr. Hyde.

Krohn, Wylie and Ragsdale, in conjunction, determined Hollman medically and psychologically had "a defect causing a split personality." Their medical and neurological conclusions were issued to the press for publication.

"He (Hollman) had two different natures," the New York Times reported.

William O. Krohn wrote that the abnormalities he found in Hollman's brain "resemble that of the more noted criminals, such as McElvain executed by electricity at Sing Sing, New York."

Charles McElvain was 19-years-old when he brutally murdered Christian W. Lucea, a Brooklyn, New York grocer on August 22, 1889. McElvain broke into a storeroom and had stabbed the man to death. He was convicted of first degree murder and sentenced to die by Electrocution.

During his stay at Sing Sing, McElvain earned the reputation of being "the toughest prisoner" there. He reportedly told another prisoner executed before him, "Goodbye, damn you! You'll be in hell before I am."

Before he died on February 8, 1892, Charles McElvain had a Christian conversion, much like Frederick Hollman. At the moment of his execution, McElvain was reported to have cried out, "Oh Jesus, help me! Oh, my God, help me and save me! Oh, Christ, help me!" It was said to be the man's final words.

Concerning the examination of Hollman's brain, Krohn wrote, "it is the brain of one of the greatest degenerates that has ever lived among men; the brain of an individual who stands as a monster outside the pale of civilization."

Hollman's brain, which weighed fifty-two ounces, Krohn reported "differs in many aspects from a normal brain." Through careful "microscopic" examination he came to some startling conclusions.

The examination revealed on the posterior section or the cerebellum had noticeable defects of protrusion. A regular sigmoid line in a normal brain was found to be broken, irregular and "entirely out of form."

"It is the typical brain of a born criminal," Krohn wrote. "It in no sense is a normal brain and certain characteristics compel one to call it the brain of a degenerate. From Hollman's history, one is compelled to believe that so far as one side of his nature was concerned, he was a homicidal novice maniac."

According Krohn, to the very last moment Hollman's vanity remained as a marked mental characteristic.

"In a hundred ways, Hollman showed his supreme conceit, yet at the same time his other self was engrossed in citing scripture, humming religious hymns, and indulging in prayer and incantations," Krohn wrote.

The skull of Frederick Hollman was preserved and used for many years as a prop in Professor Krohn's psychology class at the University of Illinois.

"Professor Krohn used the brain and skull for certain demonstrations before his class in psychology," a Chicago Postgraduate Medical School report was quoted in the North American Practitioner journal.

University critics of Krohn claimed his "interest in abnormal psychology" had attracted students out of "morbid curiosity."

Where the skull is today, or if it still exists, is unknown. It could still be on a dusty shelf in the archives at the University of Illinois.

PART 9

Investigation, Examination, and
Mission for Justice

In the days after Frederick Hollman's execution, scattershot information began to be published in newspapers regarding "cold case" files. It came from areas where Hollman had lived involving unsolved murders of German women that had occurred.

The most high profile claim came from authorities in Hanover, Pennsylvania, which was a German settlement.

Three days after Hollman's execution, the May 17, 1897 edition of the Grand Haven Tribune republished a news article from another paper that reported authorities in Pennsylvania were reinvestigating a murder that took place there a year and a half earlier.

"Within the last few days another murder has been laid at the door of (Frederick) Hollman committed in Hanover Pennsylvania, in November 1895," the Tribune wrote. "He (Hollman) was near there at the time under the (assumed) name of Fred Lang. Hollman was lucky in evading consequences of his misdeeds and with great cunning covered up every crime."

The item reported that those who knew Hollman "when he resided there" near Hanover spoke of his dual nature.

"He (Hollman) spoke but little and had no intimates," the Tribune relayed. "He worked but a short time at any one job and in the summertime spent most of his time fishing."

Little more could be discovered concerning this murder even with the assistance of the Hanover Historical Society.

Authorities in several locations where Hollman had worked and lived were reopening unsolved murder cases. They focused on Hollman's method of strangulation and victims that were left hanging with twine from doorknobs.

With Frederick Hollman dead and leaving no public confession, no one can ever be sure how many victims died at his hands. Some newspapers speculated a few unsolved murders in Indiana and Michigan, which occurred during Hollman's killing spree, could have been attributed to him.

An article published on May 14, 1897 in the Warsaw Daily Times in Indiana, suggested Hollman might have murdered as many as 17 women.

"From 1893 on there were a number of suspicious deaths of women in the vicinity of where he (Hollman) was, but none attributed to him until his arrest last December," the Warsaw Daily Times reported. The newspaper relayed besides Wiebke Geddes and "four other women," Hollman "almost certainly" had murdered "perhaps a dozen others."

A crime-suspense magazine called *Intimate Detective Stories*, which published a dramatized account of the Hollman murders in July 1945, stated that Hollman had "confessed to all murders" attributed to him.

The piece, presented as a "special investigation" written by Jack Clements, bore some remarkable facts that only a researcher could know. However, it delved into embellishment, rearranged events and locations, and manufactured a great deal of dialog.

Clearly based on the case rather than being a record of it, the piece presented a quote attributed to Hollman where he confessed to a murder he committed in his native country.

"I killed an old woman near Ombrau, in Germany," Hollman reportedly said. "It was a great joke when the police asked me to help them search."

If there was any truth to this element of the story, it was a murder Hollman would have committed before he arrived in America in 1883.

The May 21, 1897 edition of the Weekly Call of Troy, Illinois, reported "men who followed the (Hollman) case feel positive (he had committed) at least a dozen murders." The newspaper also published an item unseen in other press reports that "innocent men have been hanged" for Hollman's crimes. The source of this information is unknown.

Only two of the three states where Hollman was reported to have committed murder had a death penalty, Illinois and Pennsylvania. Wisconsin did not. Between this pair, in 1895, 1896 and up to Hollman's execution in 1897, a total of 16 men were hanged for the crime of murder. Of those convictions, only a few involved a female victim. In those cases, only one man, charged with killing his wife, claimed he was innocent. The woman had been shot using a pistol, a weapon Hollman was not known to own or carry.

After Hollman's death, his defense attorney Columbus Schneider revealed that his client had "confessed" to him only one murder, that of Alberta Hilgendorf.

Information about the "confession" was made public by Schneider only because Alberta Hilgendorf's husband had been convicted of her murder, and he saw no reason to uphold any client-attorney confidentiality agreement since Hollman was dead.

Two days after Hollman's execution, and likely the day of his burial in Glen Cemetery in Illinois, his former church, St. Paul's Evangelical Lutheran church of Grand Haven, laid the cornerstone for their new building. Services had been conducted elsewhere until this point.

Frederick Hollman's cousin Charlie Hallman was there with his family for the groundbreaking.

Three days after Hollman's execution, the Grand Haven Tribune published a brief commentary regarding the killer. The short editorial was written by Tribune publisher Horace G. Nichols.

"For a town of it size, Grand Haven is not slow when it comes to producing characters in the sensational world," Nichols wrote. "One of our citizens (Frederick Hollman) has but recently won the distinction of being legally executed."

To this day, Frederick Hollman remains the only resident of Grand Haven who was ever executed for a crime.

Kevin Collier

Professor William O. Krohn's initial psychological examination of Frederick Hollman appeared in many newspapers about a week after the killer's execution.

The most complete evaluation of Hollman written by Professor Krohn was in an article titled "Psychological Analysis of Frederick Hollman," which was published in the 1903 book "The Criminal Classes: Causes and Cures," compiled by Daniel Right Miller.

According to Krohn, Hollman was both "a brute and murderer as well as a religious enthusiast."

In Krohn's analysis he outlined that "no less than five murders and at least eight different attempts at murder" were attributed to Hollman. And while the killer possessed a horrendous evil side, there was also a spiritual demeanor in the man as well.

During most of Hollman's incarceration in the Ford County jailhouse, he sang hymns and read scripture.

"He was very proud of his Bible," Krohn wrote. "On it inscribed in gold letters was, 'as for me and my house, we will serve the Lord.' This he carefully held toward the camera when his picture was taken on the scaffold."

During Krohn's observation of Hollman leading up to the execution, he noted that he was offended by killer's "arrogant vanity."

This behavior revealed itself especially in regards to the murderer's granted request for a glass pane coffin lid.

It was determined Hollman had two personalities as a result of manifested neuropathic symptoms which, according to Krohn, caused him to inherit "some nervous taint."

"This perhaps made it impossible to inhibit his violent outbreaks of passion, both spiritual and criminal," Krohn wrote.

Hollman had a side described as "tenderly sentimental, emotional and religious," one newspaper reported. This demeanor always concerned his life with first wife Amelia.

"Ordinarily, he seemed a simple German farm hand," a New York Times article explained. "But he could become enraged easily, and it was said that you wouldn't want to set him off."

It was reported Hollman never displayed any remorse for his violent and murderous acts.

Krohn's psychological examination noted that his violent behavior and methods of gripping women in the throat with intent to murder them had been going on for some time, and began shortly after his second marriage in 1888 to Augusta Rohde in Grand Haven.

Krohn concluded Hollman's hatred of his second wife had manifested in a hatred of all women. He had been arrested in 1890 for beating Augusta Hollman and had threatened to hang her, forcing her to watch how he would do it practicing on a dog.

"The same methods were used (hanging with binding twine) in every case, and never once did he ever exhibit remorse for his horrible misdeeds," Krohn wrote. "For seven or eight years he had been ruthlessly pursing the same fiendish course, until his crimes seemed nothing but matter of fact occurrences to him."

In June 1897, the Ford County bar, county officials, and ex-officials gave a reception in honor of retiring Judge Alfred Sample at the Middlecoff Hotel in Paxton.

Sample had presided over Hollman's murder trial.

Toasts at the occasion were numerous, with twelve persons standing to read statements in tribute to the Judge observing his 12 years on the bench.

It is said one of the reasons Judge Sample retired was because of the emotional effect the Hollman trial had on him.

The celebratory occasion, in a way, was a reunion of many key figures who had just experienced and endured the most horrific tragedy in the history of Ford County.

Featured speakers at Sample's retirement event were Hollman's prosecuting Attorney Abraham Phillips, Hollman's Defense Attorney, Columbus Schneider, and Hollman's jailer Sheriff Benjamin Mason.

Also in attendance were Weaver White, Sr., father to a Hollman trial juror and J. H. and W. S. Moffett, brothers of August Moffett, who also a juror in the Hollman trial.

Kevin Collier

Columbus Schneider's role as defender of Frederick Hollman ended with the death of his client, but the story of Hollman's victims was far from over. Hollman's "confession" to him as the killer of Bertha Hilgendorf compelled Schneider to become an advocate to exonerate August Hilgendorf.

August Hilgendorf was convicted of murdering his wife Bertha in Pleasant Prairie, Wisconsin on July 4, 1896. He remained in the state prison at Waupun.

Days after Frederick Hollman had been executed, the District Attorney in Kenosha, Wisconsin was investigating information coming out of Paxton, Illinois that an innocent man was imprisoned for the crime of murder.

Before his trial, August Hilgendorf had been demonized in the press by rumors spread by the public. One had been a claim authorities had discovered the body of another dead woman hidden beneath the porch of the Hilgendorf residence days after his wife had been murdered.

Rumor was that the additional murder victim was a niece of Bertha Hilgendorf, whom August did not like. The stories included horrid details of the fictitious killing.

"Someone with a fertile imagination started the story," the July 14, 1896 edition of the Milwaukee Journal reported. "The story is a canard."

The medical examiner who examined Bertha Hilgendorf's body, which was discovered in the milk house on the property, testified on the first day of the trial that "it was impossible for a body to fall in the position it lay."

This challenged the theory the woman had taken her own life.

August Hilgendorf had suggested her cause of death was "suicide" when he was arrested and he claimed he did not know how she died and protested any involvement.

There was never any evidence presented at Hilgendorf's trial that another man, Frederick Hollman, was in the neighborhood at the time of the murder. Nor that this man had discussed the murder with others before he left town the day after.

Hilgendorf's conviction of murder weighed heavily on his behavior the day of his wife's death.

Described as "gloriously drunk" when he discovered his wife's corpse in the milk house, Hilgendorf showed little concern. He milked cows, ate dinner and had not even bothered to cover his wife's half-nude body with a sheet.

However, Columbus Schneider knew the behavior of the husband and son of murder victim Grethe Seifkin had been even more egregious as they had left her body in the house overnight and did not notify police until the next day.

Also, authorities found no significant marks on August Hilgendorf's body at the time of his arrest. There was no physical evidence he had engaged in a violent struggle with his wife.

It was not until several months later after Hilgendorf was locked up in prison that an investigation into this "stranger," Frederick Hollman, took place.

The Milwaukee Journal published a story on May 17, 1897 that outlined a dispatch from Paxton that "contained a statement that Fred Hollman, who was executed, was the murderer of Mrs. Hilgendorf, and that her husband (August) was innocent of the crime."

The dispatch from also stated "It is certain that he (Hollman) killed Bertha Hilgendorf on July 4, 1896 near Kenosha, Wisconsin."

An initial report in the Stevens Point Journal stated in a headline Bertha Hilgendorf was "Probably killed by a tramp." The newspaper explained, "Both he (August) and a son (Bernhard) who found the murdered woman are under arrest, but many attribute the crime to tramps."

At the time of the murder of Bertha Hilgendorf Frederick Hollman was employed cutting corn for farmer who lived only one mile from the Hilgendorf residence.

Hollman had stated during this time that he "lived for a month" at the home of Henry Lang, a 48-year-old farmer in Pleasant Prairie, Wisconsin. Henry Lang lived with his wife

Henrietta, age 44, and two orphaned nephews Jacob and Henry Lang.

The Langs were friends of their fellow German Lutherans the Hilgendorfs, and likely Henry Lang was a regular patron of August Hilgendorf's saloon.

It is likely this was how Hollman became familiar with the Hilgendorfs, through Henry Lang.

Coincidentally, people in the Pleasant Prairie and Kenosha area knew Hollman by an assumed name, Fred Lang.

The May 3, 1897 edition of the Chicago Tribune reported, "His several aliases, so far known, all of which he acknowledges having used at places, (includes) Fred Lang (in) Waukesha, Somers and Kenosha County, Wisconsin."

It was reported Hollman left town the day after the murder, but not before telling neighbors near the scene that August Hilgendorf had killed his wife. Hollman had also described in detail how the woman had been murdered.

"Nearly everybody now agrees that (August) Hilgendorf is the innocent creature of circumstances," The Middleville Sun, Michigan newspaper reported on May 20, 1897.

During the time of Hollman's incarceration at the Ford County jailhouse awaiting trial, the Kenosha District Attorney Albert E. Buckmaster said that the dispatch "failed to reveal a claim of truth" and "the story is not given credence here."

The investigation was suspended as it could not be determined what the certainty was, as the evidence was circumstantial.

Eight months after Hollman's execution, the St. Paul Minnesota Globe newspaper published an article on January 29, 1898 concerning the murder of Bertha Albertine Hilgendorf.

The story voiced concern over whether Bertha Hilgendorf's husband was an innocent man as strong circumstantial evidence pointed to Hollman as the true killer.

Another investigation followed, which was conducted by District Attorney Albert E. Buckmaster and resulted in no exoneration for August Hilgendorf.

Buckmaster again determined Hollman could not have committed the murder.

According to the St. Paul Minnesota Globe article, Columbus Schneider had come from Paxton, Illinois to Kenosha, Wisconsin to bring the case before Governor Edward Scofield to see if it was possible to "secure a pardon for (August) Hilgendorf."

The article revealed in print "Attorney C. S. Schneider, of Paxton, claims that Hollman made a confession to him of this murder."

If Schneider's claim that Hollman confessed to him in private under the lawyer-client privilege to the murder of Bertha Hilgendorf, it is possible Hollman had confessed to all of the murders attributed to him.

The theory is supported by what Schneider wrote published in the Grand Haven Tribune on April 24, 1897. It was before Hollman's execution. Schneider had stated, "I am convinced that he is guilty."

The Melvin Transcript published an article in their May 21, 1897 edition exonerating August Hildendorf.

"August Hilgendorf, condemned to drag out the rest of his life in the Waupun, Wisconsin penitentiary for the murder of his wife, can see a glimmer of sunshine," the Illinois newspaper wrote. "Hollman expiated (to make amends; atone for) that very crime on the gallows, and that Hilgendorf is the innocent."

More evidence supporting the exoneration of August Hilgendorf came in the fall of that year with a sworn statement by a Wisconsin State Prison inmate in Waupun who had been a cellmate of Hollman in early 1897.

The witness' name was William Kelly.

William Kelly had been arrested and lodged at the Ford County jailhouse in Illinois from mid-January to Mid-April for stealing a turkey. While there, Kelly befriended Frederick Hollman.

Kelly said Hollman had made a confession to him that "he had killed" Bertha Hilgendorf with an accomplice named Baltimore Shorty and that her husband (August Hilgendorf) had been convicted of the crime and was serving a life sentence.

An April 1897 issue of The Paxton Record confirms William Kelly was there at the Ford County jailhouse serving a sentence while awaiting trial.

"William Kelly, of Gibson City, convicted burglary and larceny of stealing chickens and turkeys from Thomas Crowe of Dix Township," the Paxton Record printed in a list of prisoners at trial. "Verdict, guilty. Motion for new trial."

At the time Hollman reportedly spoke to his cellmate about the Hilgendorfs, Kelly had not read or heard anything about the murder of Bertha Hilgendorf nor the conviction of her husband for the crime.

"I knew nothing of the case," Kelly stated, until Hollman spoke to him about it.

William Kelly had spoken of Hollman's jailhouse confession to authorities previously, but apparently was ignored. In November 1898 the claim was taken seriously when Kelly wrote a sworn, signed statement that was witnessed by Joseph McClaughry, Warden of the Wisconsin State Prison.

"He's simply an ignorant, loutish fellow without full appreciation of property rights," Warden McClaughry described Kelly. McClaughry noted Kelly had lived most of his life in Fond du Lac, Wisconsin. "He's not dangerous."

In the statement, William Kelly calls Hollman "Hartman," which was the name he had given when he was arrested for murder of Wiebke Geddes on December 6, 1896.

Kelly's letter, dated November 29, 1898, read:

I was an inmate of the Ford county, Illinois, jail during a part of January, all February, March and part of April, 1897, during which time I was the close friend of Fred Hartman.

About March 18 or 19, a date I recall on account of the arrest of two men on St. Patrick's day, Hartman stated to me than an "old Dutch farmer was doing life in Wisconsin for a job he and a man known as Baltimore Shorty had done." He wanted to ask the men arrested if they knew Shorty.

He said the name of the man doing life in Wisconsin was Hilgendorf or Higgendorf. Hartman said if his wife knew where he was she knew enough to hang him.

227

He said his wife lived in Wisconsin. Hartman was at the time awaiting trial for the murder of a woman. He was afterward hanged at Paxton, Ill., on May 14, 1897. I make this statement of my own accord and without promise of favor, reward or assistance of any kind.

Signed, William Kelly.

Witness: J. R. McClaughry, Warden.

The sworn statement, when deciphered, reveals two compelling points.

Hollman wanted to ask the two men who were arrested around St. Patrick's Day and lodged in the Ford County jailhouse if they knew his friend "Baltimore Shorty," lending credence to the existence of the man.

Whether Hollman had an accomplice in the murder of Bertha Hilgendorf is unknown. It is only in Kelly's statement that "Baltimore Shorty," likely a nick-name, is even mentioned.

The two men arrested around St. Patrick's Day and lodged in the Ford County jailhouse were said to be tramps, brothers John and Henry Harris, both of Chicago. One received a prison sentence, the other 30 days in jail.

Kelly's statement reveals Hollman's admission that he was a killer.

Kelly wrote Hollman had remarked, "If his wife knew where he was she knew enough to hang him."

It meant if Frederick Hollman's wife Augusta knew he was in jail and charged with murder, "she knew enough" (personally) that he was guilty and should be executed. Hollman had threatened to hang his wife and showed her how he would do it by stringing up a dog.

A few weeks after Frederick Hollman's execution, a former bartender named Carl Kreebe, age 25 from Washington, Illinois, came forward with information concerning an encounter he had with Hollman in the fall of 1896.

Kreebe, a German who had owned a saloon in Gilman, saw Hollman's picture in a news article at the time of his execution, which prompted him to contact authorities.

Kreebe told the Piper City Journal that one night Hollman "got drunk in the bar" and became loose lipped revealing a shocking past.

"He told me of having committed crimes upon women and girls in Wisconsin far more atrocious than murder," Kreebe said.

Hollman and Kreebe were reportedly alone in the saloon and the disclosure was said in confidence.

"He said he dared not go back where he committed the crimes or the farmers would put a rope around his neck," Kreebe added.

Nothing transpired in August Hilgendorf's favor when news of Hollman's jailhouse confession to William Kelly surfaced in the pages Illinois and Wisconsin newspapers the end of 1898.

The Milwaukee Journal published an article about Hilgendorf's proclaimed innocence on May 13, 1901, almost 4 years to the day of Frederick Hollman's execution. Friends of Hilgendorf and family had filed a petition with Wisconsin Governor Robert La Follette, Sr. asking his to grant a pardon for the convicted man.

Newspapers covering the appeal for a pardon reported that Hollman "declared that he, and not Hilgendorf killed the old woman."

"The man who confessed to the crime was in the neighborhood of the Hilgendorf farm at the time of the murder." The Milwaukee Journal reported. "Hilgendorf always protested his innocence and was found guilty largely on circumstantial evidence."

The Milwaukee Journal added that Hilgendorf had been "a model prisoner and has been constantly urging his friends to establish his innocence."

Hilgendorf's defenders had somewhat embellished the tale of the facts known at the time of his arrest and perceived. This compelled a re-examination by Governor La Follette of the known facts and the case was briefly reopened.

La Follette rendered a determination that there was "no evidence" Hollman "had ever confessed" to the murder of Bertha Hilgendorf to anyone.

Apparently, it did not matter if Columbus Schneider and a convict named William Kelly were saying it was true.

There is no evidence attorney Columbus Schneider was ever hired to represent August Hilgendorf during the appeal for his freedom. It appears Schneider bore the expense of what became a personal six year crusade.

The efforts of Columbus Schneider and others failed, and Hilgendorf was never released.

PART 10

The People Hollman Left Behind

Frederick Hollman's wife Augusta remained in Green Lake County and Fond du Lac, Wisconsin until her death in 1945.

After Frederick Hollman abandoned her in January 1892, she generally lived in poverty raising her two children, Minnie and Herman. She became a domestic servant and often took in the laundry of others to make ends meet.

Her sister, Albertine, whom Augusta came to America with in 1887, married Miller (Mueller) Miller on July 25, 1899. The couple lived in a farmhouse in nearby Neshkoro. They, along with extended family and friends at St. John's Evangelical Lutheran Church, helped Augusta when in need.

By 1900 Augusta and her children boarded at the residence of John Johnson, a widowed 71-year-old Englishman. Augusta was employed as a servant and housekeeper.

A joyous event transpired on May 2, 1902 when Augusta's mother, Anna Karoline Rohde, age 67 and widowed, arrived in America. She brought with her a daughter, Martha and her husband Julius Gustav Selchow. Augusta's sister Albertine and her husband Fredrick Miller paid for and arranged for their passage to America.

Another happy moment was when Augusta remarried on February 3, 1903, taking Herman Henry Albert Boettcher as her second husband. They were married by Reverend John August Hoyer at Evangelical Lutheran Church in Princeton.

Boettcher, born in Germany in 1870, was a blacksmith by trade and owned a shop on W. Fond du Lac Street. Boettcher came to America as a young man with his parents, and lived in Minnesota before moving to Wisconsin.

Herman and Augusta Boettcher, with children Herman and Minnie Hollman, resided in a little white house on Hamburg Street in Ripon, which still stands today.

The Boettchers had two children of their own, Frieda born on January 25, 1904 and Ernest born on April 4, 1905.

Herman Boettcher assumed the role of father to Herman and Minnie Hollman, but never adopted the children.

Augusta's mother, Anna Karoline Rohde, died at the age of 79 on December 16, 1913 due to heart disease. She was buried at Dartford Cemetery in Green Lake County.

Minnie and Herman Hollman never knew what truly had happened to their birth father. Augusta told the children that their father had been killed in a railroad accident in Chicago around 1900. The fabricated story, told to protect her children from the horrible truth, would be passed on from generation to generation.

Herman and Augusta (Hollman) Boettcher were married for over 40 years until they passed away. Augusta died on January 3, 1945 at the age of 76. The Reverend W. Schlachtenhaufen officiated at her funeral.

Herman Boettcher died on November 12, 1947 at the age of 77.

Both are buried in Woodlawn Cemetery in Ripon, Wisconsin.

CHILDREN HERMAN AND MINNIE HOLLMAN

Frederick Hollman's son, Herman August Hollman, became a farmer and was veteran of World War I.

He married Anna Willie on February 28, 1920 and the two resided just outside of Ripon in a big white farmhouse. On the property stood a barn and a large metal windmill.

Herman Hollman and his wife had five daughters, Caroline, Beatrice, Audrey, Mildred, and Bernice.

Herman's wife was said to be "evil and violent," and reports have it that the couple's oldest daughter Caroline actually took care of the children.

It is said Anna was struck by a bolt of lightning while hiding under the only tree out in the middle of a farm field and afterwards was "twice as mean as before."

Herman Hollman died at the age of 68 on November 28, 1959 by committing suicide. He turned on his car in the garage and ran a hose from the exhaust pipe into the interior of the vehicle.

Some ancestors question if Anna was somehow responsible, but it is only speculation.

Herman was buried on November 30 in Woodlawn Cemetery in Ripon, Wisconsin. His wife, Anna, passed away in 1966, and is buried beside him.

Frederick Hollman's last surviving child, Minnie Augusta Hollman, married Frank W. Wilke in 1908.

Wilke was born on Oct. 17, 1873 in Wisconsin.

Frank and Minnie endured poverty and hardship moving often in the Green Lake and Fond du Lac area to find odd jobs to make ends meet.

Frank worked for a time in a cranberry bog, and the two were employed for a time at an apple orchard. Minnie walked to work six miles one way when she held a job at a canning factory.

The couple had five children, Mildred, Henry, John, Eddie, and Margaret.

In 1920 the family lived in Winnebago. They also resided in Eureka for a time but had to move when their home burned down.

Frank broke his hip in a fall and could do little after that. It was said Minnie did not have enough money to travel to the hospital during his recovery. Then Frank contracted pneumonia after cutting trees with another man during winter and died in January 1943 at the age of 69.

After her husband's death, Minnie had a home in Berlin, Wisconsin and in later years lived in a little cottage at 114 Forest Avenue in Fond du Lac. She would wake in the middle of the night to put wood in the stove to keep the house warm.

In her final years she resided at an apartment on Military Road before moving into a nursing home.

Minnie Hollman Wilke died on March 3, 1981 at the age of 92 and was buried beside her husband Frank in Oakwood Cemetery in Berlin, Wisconsin.

Ancestors still fondly and affectionately recall moments they shared with Minnie, calling her "a sweetheart."

The last surviving grandchild of Frederick Hollman was Mildred, daughter of Frank and Minnie Wilke. Mildred Martha (Wilke) Sorenson was born on August 24, 1911 and died on January 14, 2004.

While great grandchildren of Frederick Hollman survive today, no descendants carried on the Hollman name.

MINNIE HOLLMAN-WILKE'S SON AND GRANDSON

Minnie Hollman-Wilke's grandson James Perry Wilke, born on March 8, 1957, became a murderer 100 years after his infamous great-grandfather Frederick Hollman's killing spree began.

Minnie and Frank Wilke's son John, age 69, was gunned down and killed by his eldest son James on August 3, 1996 after returning to his Royal Oak, Michigan home from the market on a Saturday morning.

James Perry Wilke, age 39, who lived with his parents, then chased his 67-year-old mother Arlene as she fled the house and shot her to death near the street.

Neighbors who heard the shots and witnessed Arlene's murder called for police. James turned the gun on himself and committed suicide in the backyard of the home just as authorities arrived.

Unknown to the extended family at the time, James suffered most of his life from the mental health disorder Schizophrenia.

The news of the massacre made the front page of the Royal Oak News Detroit News and Free Press, Michigan.

HOLLMAN'S BROTHER, JULIUS HALLMAN

It is unknown what became of Frederick Hollman's brother Julius, who went by the last name of Hallman and lived in Ripon, Wisconsin.

Seeking funds for his attorney pending his trial, Frederick Hollman claimed Julius owed him $300, but was unable to make contact with his sibling.

There was a Herman "Julius" Hallman, who was born on Brandenburg, Germany in August 4, 1864 and immigrated to America settling first in Green Lake County, Wisconsin. A farmer by trade, this man moved to the town of Newton in Marquette County where he married in November 1895 and had seven children.

However, census records indicate his father's first name was not Charles. But the Hollman family of the period often interchanged their first and middle names.

The most convincing evidence this was Frederick Hollman's brother "Julius" comes from a photographic comparison of the two. Pictures of Herman "Julius" Hallman bear a remarkable and compelling likeness to photos and drawings of Frederick Hollman.

"Julius" Hallman died on June 21, 1935 and was buried in St. Paul's Lutheran Church Cemetery Newton Township, Marquette County, Wisconsin.

HOLLMAN'S COUSIN, CHARLIE HALLMAN

Charlie Hallman, Frederick Hollman's cousin who lived in Grand Haven, raised eight children with his wife Augusta, seven of whom can be identified by the first names of William, Minnie, Frank, Edward, Emily, Martha, and Albert.

Three of the daughters married and became Mrs. John Fisher, Mrs. Rupert E. Hall and Mrs. G. E. Delong. One daughter, Martha, never married.

Charlie Hallman enjoyed a distinguished life among the German community of Grand Haven.

Hallman was elected a trustee for the German Workingman's Society in August 1894, active in workman's rights and was a founding member of St. Paul's Evangelical Lutheran Church, of which, he and his wife were lifelong members.

Hallman was employed as a car inspector for the Grand Trunk Railway for some four decades.

Charlie's wife, Augusta Hallman, passed away in October 14, 1918. The Grand Haven Tribune called her a "highly respected" member of the community. She reportedly had two sisters who lived in Grand Haven at the time of her death, Mrs. J. Mordrock and Mrs. W. Strahsburg.

With his wife's passing, Charlie Hallman retired from his job with the Grand Trunk Railway and moved to Milwaukee, Wisconsin to live with his son-in-law John Fisher and his daughter.

As adults, Charlie Hallman's children moved around the country residing in New York, Chicago, Boston and Milwaukee. Edward was stationed in Honolulu and served in the United States Army during World War I.

Charlie Hallman passed away on August 2, 1937 at the age of 83. In his obituary, he was called a "pioneer" resident of Grand Haven.

Services were held at Van Zantwick Funeral Home with the Reverend John Clemens officiating. Pallbearers were John McCracken, Herman Kohberg, Tony Ver Hoeks, Fred Brown, Hamilton Boyd, and Emil Kluempel.

Charlie Hallman and his wife are both buried in Lake Forest Cemetery in Grand Haven, Michigan.

Another cousin of Frederick Hollman, Carl Hallman, presumed a brother to Charlie who also lived in Grand Haven when Frederick resided there, was said to have moved from Grand Haven with his wife and children out east.

DEFENSE ATTORNEY, JUDGE, SHERIFF, PROSECUTOR, GUARDS AND UNDERTAKER

Frederick Hollman's attorney, Columbus S. Schneider, born in Cincinnati, Ohio on December 22, 1868, ran for political office several times and was elected to the Illinois House of Representatives (D) for the 17th District.

Schneider and his wife Mattie rubbed elbows with many nationally elected government officials and once attended an inaugural ball for President Franklin Roosevelt. Schneider passed away on February 27, 1942 at the age of 73. He was buried in Glen Cemetery in Ford County, Illinois.

The presiding judge in Frederick Hollman's trail, Alfred Sample, is also buried in Glen Cemetery, as is Ford County Sheriff Benjamin Franklin Mason.

Judge Sample retired a month after the Hollman trial in June 1897. It was said his retirement had to do with the horrific nature of the case.

He died after a year-long illness on June 11, 1902 at the age of 55.

Sheriff Benjamin Mason, who was Frederick Hollman's jailer and one of the closest persons to the condemned man, was so emotionally affected by the experience he did not seek another term as Sheriff.

Mason retired in 1898 and passed away in 1904 at the age of 71.

Abraham Lincoln Phillips, Illinois State Attorney who prosecuted Hollman for the murder of Wiebke Geddes, continued his legal career in Illinois.

Born in Lostant, Illinois on July 2, 1862, he passed away at the age of 83 on October 22, 1945 and was buried at Graceland Cemetery in Chicago.

Laurence E. Campbell, who served as Hollman's death watch guard and companion, raised children Orville and Joseph in Ford County with his wife Jennie.

Laurence and Jennie retired to Pine Bluff, Arkansas later in life, and enjoyed a marriage of 37 years.

Laurence Campbell died on April 28, 1939, his wife passed away on April 18, 1942. They are buried in Bellwood Annex Cemetery, in Jefferson County, Arkansas.

Charles C. Houdyshell, who also served as Frederick Hollman's guard during his time at the Ford County jailhouse, died of a stroke on April 20, 1907 while on patrol. Houdyshell was 71-years-old. He is buried in Drummer Township Cemetery.

Ivis Luke Atwood, who built Hollman's infamous coffin featuring the glass viewing pane, went on to establish an undertaking parlor besides being proprietor of a furniture business. Atwood died in 1946 at the age of 84 and is buried in Glen Cemetery beside his wife, Susan.

TALE OF THREE JURORS

During Frederick Hollman's trial he reportedly asked Sheriff Benjamin Mason for his pistol so that he "could shoot and kill the jurors."

All 12 jurors survived the trial, but three of them, in particular, are worth noting.

Two of the jurors, who lived very long lives, were Augustus A. Moffett and Henry Lindgren. Both are buried in Glen Cemetery in Ford County, Illinois.

Henry Lindgren, a farmer who was born in 1858 lived to be 93, passing away on December 11, 1952. He was also the final juror from the trial to die.

Augustus A. Moffett, a day laborer, born in 1848, passed away at the age of 97 of in 1945. He was the oldest juror to die.

Another juror, William Wallace Reser, a farmer, died on June 21, 1917 after suffering a stroke after he cut his lawn at the age of 43. One of Reser's grandsons, Gustaf Albert Kingren, briefly dated the former Maureen Schneider in the 1950s, which created an interesting coincidence.

Maureen Schneider was the daughter of Frederick Hollman's defense attorney, Columbus Schnieder. Schneider was a divorcee, and Kingren was recently widowed. Thus, the daughter of Hollman's attorney dated the grandson of one of the jurors that sentenced him to Hollman to death.

THE HECKENS BROTHERS

Julius Claus Heckens, the youngest person to give testimony at the trial of Frederick Hollman, was also one of the first witnesses to die.

One of five children born to Claus and Anna Maria Heckens of Drummer Township, Julius, age 12, and his brother Peter, age 5, encountered Hollman on a the road while heading home from Ashley schoolhouse on December 1, 1896, the day before Wiebke Geddes was murdered.

On the morning of the murder, Heckens went to the schoolhouse to light a fire in the woodstove and found one already going. He noticed someone had stayed there overnight and that the key to the building was missing.

Julius, born June 2, 1884, was living with his sister Bertie and her husband Ray Morrison in North Dakota at the time he came down with typhoid fever. He died of an intestinal hemorrhage on May 2, 1907 at the age of 22.

Peter Heckens was in the company of his older brother Julius when they encountered Frederick Hollman on the road. Born April 1891, Peter died on October 22, 1961 at the age of 69. Peter's wife was the former Augusta Stroh, a member of the Stroh family, who owned the property were the Geddes family lived. Peter and his brother Julius are buried in Drummer Township Cemetery in Gibson City, Illinois.

Henry William Heckens, born in May of 1881, was one of the persons who showed up at the Stuhmer farmhouse on December 6, 1896 to guard against Hollman fleeing the location before Constable Ira Gilmore and authorities arrived to arrest the suspect. Henry Heckens, age 15 at the time, died in 1947 at the age of 66. He and his wife Elsie had several children.

HOLLMAN'S COUNSELOR, PROFESSOR BLOME

Rudolph Harin Heinrich Blome of the Rice Collegiate Institute at Paxton moved his family, wife Mary Jane and four children, to back to Germany soon after Hollman's execution. While there he attended the University of Jena.

Blome was born in Germany in 1854.

In 1900, Blome was awarded the degree of doctor of philosophy and returned with his family to the United States. He assumed a teaching position in psychology at Illinois State University.

Blome's experience with Frederick Hollman undoubtedly motivated him to further his career in psychology and philosophy. There can be little doubt during his lifetime Blome would never encounter a case the magnitude of Frederick Hollman again.

Blome next accepted a teaching position at Tempe Normal School and was promoted to president of Northern Arizona Normal School in 1909. He immediately brought to the campus a sense of professionalism, initiative, and enthusiasm.

Under Blome's leadership, a multitude of academic and recreational student activities were developed, including interscholastic sports. The number of students attending classes rose from sixty-eight to more than three hundred. Blome expanded the facilities to accommodate the growth.

Despite all his accomplishments, Blome was forced to leave his position as president of Northern Arizona Normal School under unfortunate circumstances. A victim of the anti-German hysteria associated with World War I, Blome encountered hostility toward his German birth from a few politically placed individuals.

For months, Flagstaff residents and the student body rallied against Blome's removal; however, politics prevailed, and Blome was dismissed in the spring of 1918.

Blome found employment as the principal of Bisbee High School and in 1919 became director of vocational education for Arizona. In 1921, Blome moved to Pasadena, California, where he died in 1923 at the age of 69.

After remodeling in 1983, the former Training School Building in the Northern Arizona Normal School Historic District was renamed "The Blome Building" in honor of Rudolph H. H. Blome.

The Blome Building currently houses administration offices.

REVEREND GEORGE M. WILSON

In Frederick Hollman's final statement read on the morning he was executed, he gave credit to Baptist Reverend George M. Wilson for his "deliverance."

Through the Reverend Wilson's efforts I have been saved. I thank him for his kindness," Hollman wrote.

Born on August 22, 1817, George Wilson died on November 1, 1905 at the age of 85. He is buried at Evergreen Memorial Cemetery in Bloomington, McLean County, Illinois.

Engraved on his headstone from scripture is, "Them also which sleep in Jesus will God Bring with Him," 1 Thessalonians 4:14.

In a portrait and biographical album of McLean County, Illinois, published the year his wife died in 1887, it stated Wilson is a staunch Republican and early in his life, "when it was unpopular," advocated the abolition of slavery.

PROFESSOR WILLIAM O. KROHN

In recent years, Professor William O. Krohn, born in 1868, has been recognized as a pioneering psychological practitioner for his work at the Eastern Hospital for the Insane at Kankakee, Illinois.

Krohn supervised the examination of Frederick Hollman's brain after his execution.

Krohn left Eastern Hospital in 1899, entered medical school at Northwestern University in 1902, and obtained an M. D. in 1905. He practiced medicine for the remainder of his life.

Krohn wrote many books on psychology and assumed a role of testifying in many murder trials as a psychiatrist who assessed the competence of defendants.

Becoming an "expert witness" in a number of widely publicized murder trials earned him national recognition.

Krohn and associate Harold Singer wrote a book published in 1924 titled "Insanity and Law; A Treatise on Forensic Psychiatry," which was a ground-breaking work.

Krohn's most significant trail as an "expert witness" was People vs. Leopold and Loeb in 1924, defended by 67-year-old Clarence Darrow.

Nathan Freudenthal Leopold, Jr. and Richard Albert Loeb, two wealthy University of Chicago students, were charged with the kidnapping and murder of 14-year-old Robert "Bobby" Franks.

Krohn argued on the stand the accused men "were both sane," and won a three-hour confrontation with Darrow. It is said when Krohn stepped down from the stand, "Darrow had to admit defeat."

The outcome of this trial has had repercussions to this day, as Darrow popularized the notion that a defendant "might not be guilty of his crime by reason of insanity."

It was the first case of its kind seeking to excuse a killer from responsibility for this reason and the "first expert" to argue against it, defeating the notion, was Krohn.

The judge sentenced Leopold and Loeb each to life imprisonment for murder plus 99 years each for kidnapping.

Krohn died July 17, 1927 at the age of 59 in Chicago right after an expedition to Borneo for the Chicago Museum. The cause of death was pulmonary cancer.

ALBERT LENZ

Albert Lenz, born August 18, 1863, remarried after the death of his wife Caroline "Carrie" Lenz, whom Frederick Hollman was suspected of murdering. Lenz married Sophia Bankart in 1900.

Albert and Carrie Lenz had two children, Charles Albert Lenz born January 24, 1895 and Florence Lenz born June 19, 1896.

Albert and Sophia Lenz lived in Gilman, Iroquois County for the remainder of their lives. Albert operated the Lenz Motor

Company, in which the second floor was an opera house and movie theater. In 1922 he built the Palace Theater next door.

Albert Lenz died January 5, 1924 at the age of 61. Sophia died on March 7, 1923.

Florence Lenz married Ernest Oliver Schmid on February 3, 1924. They took over operating the Palace Theater that same year.

One of their children, Charles E. Schmid, born December 31, 1924, operated the family business, the Palace Theatre starting in 1961.

Charles Schmid once served as deputy sheriff of Iroquois County and was a three-term mayor of Gilman. He sold the family business to son Bret Schmid for $1 in 1986. Charles passed away at the age of 73 in 1998.

Bret Schmid renovated the establishment founded by his great-grandfather Albert Lenz and in 1988 reopened the Palace Theater as The Pizza Place restaurant.

The two children born to Albert and Carrie Lenz died four years apart. Charles Albert Lenz died in 1977 and Florence Lenz-Schimd in 1981.

Albert's brother, Julius Lenz, who testified at the Hollman murder trial, died on March 3, 1925 at the age of 59.

FRED AND ELIZABETH GEDDES

Fred Geddes, whose wife Wiebke Geddes was murdered by Frederick Hollman on December 2, 1896, remarried in 1899. He made his residence with his second wife, Helen, in Wall Township in Ford County, Illinois.

Geddes' handicapped daughter Elizabeth, who had witnessed the brutal murder of her mother and herself had been choked by Hollman during the killing, passed away in 1905 at the age of 14 due to complications of her disability.

Elizabeth Geddes is buried in Melvin Cemetery in Ford County, Illinois.

Fred and Helen Geddes had as many as five children. The first born was Andrew A. Geddes in 1900, followed by Gerald

F. Geddes born in 1905, Mildred B. Geddes born in 1907, Alice C. Geddes born in 1909, and a child born in 1910.

Records indicate that in 1920 Fred and Helen Geddes were still residing in Ford County and by 1930 were living in Milwaukee, Wisconsin. Also living at their residence at that time were daughters Mildred and Alice. Also residing at the Geddes residence was married to Raymond Ryan, the husband of Alice.

The trail of the Geddes leaves off there.

There is a record of a Fred Geddes passing away on June 12, 1938 in Chicago, but it is unknown if this was the same man.

GEDDES' LANDLORD, JOHN STROH, SR.

John Stroth, Sr., the Geddes' landlord and owner of property on which their house stood, lived for 21 years after the murder of tenant Wiebke Geddes.

Born Johann Frederich Stroh on July 27, 1844 in Weddinghusen, Holstein, Germany, Stroh came to American in 1873 settling near Bloomington, Illinois. He purchased his own farm a few years later. Stroh remained on his farm until his death March 8, 1918.

Stroh and his wife Margaret (Rasmussen) Stroh had eight children, four boys and four girls, most of who continued reside McLean County, Illinois into adulthood. He contracted typhoid fever in 1905 and never fully recovered from the effects of the affliction.

Reportedly, Stroh was able to be up and about most of the time until the last few months of his life, during which heart trouble caused him much suffering. Stroh passed peacefully at the age of 73.

Coincidentally, Wiebke Geddes is buried in the same cemetery which is the final resting place for most members of the Stroh family, St. John's Lutheran Church Cemetery in the city of Anchor, McLean County, Illinois.

They were all members of the same church.

AUGUST HILGENDORF'S SONS

August Hilgendorf's sons, William, Bernhard, and Oscar, went to their graves with the knowledge that their father had been convicted of killing their mother Bertha on July 4, 1896 at their farmhouse in Pleasant Prairie, Wisconsin.

Frederick Hollman had confessed to having killed Bertha Hilgendorf to Ford County jail cellmate William Kelly and to his defense attorney, Columbus Schneider.

August Hilgendorf died at the Wisconsin State Prison in Waupun on February 19, 1903 after serving over six years.

On July 4, 1896, Bernhard Hilgendorf and his brother Oscar found their father intoxicated while enjoying early Fourth of July festivities in Kenosha and brought him home, then departed. August discovered his wife's lifeless body in the milk house on the property. Bernhard was brought in by police the day of the murder, then released.

Oscar and he had both testified at their father's murder trial.

Bernard, born in 1870, remained a farm laborer for the remainder of his life. He never married and died in 1938.

Oscar Hilgendorf, born on January 23, 1879, went on to work as a shipping clerk. He married Elenora (Kludt), who was a dressmaker at home. She died in 1923. Oscar Hilgendorf remarried in 1924, taking Emma Lublow as his second wife. Oscar fathered 3 children. He died on July 20, 1933.

William Hilgendorf, born on October 16, 1865, who was married at the time of his mother's murder, was a yard clerk for the Milwaukee Road railroad. He was wed to Margaretha Ulmer and their marriage endured 61 years. They had two children, both who died before 1900. William died on June 4, 1949.

All three Hilgendorf brothers are buried next to their parents in Union Cemetery, Milwaukee, Wisconsin.

GRETHE SEIFKIN'S HUSBAND AND SON

Mathias Seifkin, the second husband of Grethe Seifkin who was found murdered on June 13, 1896, operated a shoe repair store in Sibley after his wife's death.

He stepped on a nail in 1907 and lockjaw resulted, causing his death on November 3 at the age of 56. His burial took place in Mount Hope Cemetery, in Sibley, Illinois.

Anton H. Wolken Jr., the son of Grethe Seifkin by her first marriage, was born February 20, 1870 in Germany. After the death of his father Henry Wolken in 1888, he immigrated to America with his mother in 1889. Anton was one of six siblings who were beneficiaries from the sale of their father's homestead in Germany. His mother had divided the money among her children.

Anton Wolken married Elizabeth Johnson March 18, 1889 in Ford County. Anton and his wife had 5 children.

Wolken did not contribute a penny to his mother's burial, believing she had committed suicide. Reportedly, he refused to "bear the cost" of her burial.

It is unknown how Anton H. Wolken reacted when he discovered six months after the death of his mother that she had, in fact, been murdered.

Elizabeth Wolken died on September 15, 1907. Anton remarried shortly after, taking Martha Johnson, his deceased wife's sister, as his second wife.

Anton Wolken died sometime after 1920. He was living in Chatsworth in Livingston County at the time. His namesake son, Anton Wolken II, born in 1905, died in 1997 in Ogle, Illinois.

HOLLMAN'S FRIEND, ELIZA C. CAMPBELL

Eliza C. Campbell, a widow whom the press called "a woman who did not rank high in public estimation," was said to be a friend of Frederick Hollman and once had her picture taken with him, which she displayed in her Bloomington home.

Campbell was born Elizabeth Harvey on January 29, 1829 in Pennsylvania. Eliza had been married to Robert R. Campbell, who died on January 9, 1888. The couple had several children, two which were survivors at the time of her death, William and Edward.

Police reportedly found a "nickel" or "silver" ladies wrist watch owned by murder victim Carrie Lenz in her possession. It was said Frederick Hollman had given it to her as a gift. It was also discovered Hollman at one time had used her address as being his own. She was not believed to have known about or have been involved in any of Hollman's crimes.

Eliza Campbell passed away on March 9, 1910 at the age of 81. She is buried in Evergreen Memorial Cemetery in McLean County, Illinois.

WOMAN HOLLMAN SAID "OUGHT TO BE KILLED"

During testimony at murder trial, witness Hank Stuhmer spoke of a conversation he had with Frederick Hollman days before his arrest in which Hollman had stated he knew a woman who "ought to be killed."

"When he heard about Mrs. Geddes being killed he said there were some women who ought to be killed," Stuhmer testified. He inquired who those women might be, and Stuhmer said, "he named me a woman. (Hollman said) Herman Defries wife."

Herman Defries, born in 1864, lived in Melvin with his wife Anna M. Defries, born in 1868.

Stuhmer said Hollman told him, "(That) woman wasn't worth more than enough to be killed." Hollman added Anna Defries, like some other wives he knew, were "mean women."

Whether Anna M. Defries would have become a victim of Hollman's if he had not been caught on December 6, 1896 will never be known. But Hollman did want her dead.

Anna Defries died at the age of 55 on October 26, 1916 and is buried beside her husband in Melvin Cemetery. Herman passed away in 1940. The couple had at least six children.

Attack Survivor Mary Elizabeth Schertz

Mary Elizabeth Schertz, whom Frederick Hollman strangled in McLean County the fall of 1896 and survived the attack, lived out the remainder of her life as a single woman, never to marry. The incident reportedly took place days before the murder of Carrie Lenz.

Schertz had been choked by Hollman and escaped with the help of her brother, Peter, who was nearby when the attack occurred. According to Schertz during the attack Hollman had said "I have killed other women and I will kill you!"

Schertz identified Hollman at his jail cell the day before he was hanged.

Hollman reportedly became enraged and "threatened to kill" Schertz during her appearance.

News items published at the time named her "Lizzie" Shertz. Mary had used her middle name as her first, as her mother's name was Mary. Friends and family shortened it to Lizzie.

Mary Elizabeth Schertz was born February 18, 1873 near Stanford, Illinois, the daughter of Peter and Catherine Schertz. She had been residing with her two brothers, Daniel and Earl, on the family homestead northeast of Saybrook at the time of her death in 1942. Schertz was 69.

She is buried in Drummer Township Cemetery at Gibson City, Illinois.

Grand Haven Employer Peter Wilds

Peter Wilds employed Frederick Hollman and taught him the trade of mason in Grand Haven, Michigan. Hollman would find several jobs as brick layer with different employers up until his hanging.

Wilds, once Hollman's boss, was born in England on March 27, 1835 and arrived in America around 1860. He was a member of the 6th Michigan Calvary during the Civil War.

Peter Wilds endured a "murder mystery" of sorts in 1893 when his daughter Alice Wild turned up dead in Grand Rapids on April 17. She was one of five children from Wilds' first marriage. Effie Wilds had died on died October 24, 1880 at age 28 and Peter remarried in 1881.

Alice Wilds died during a botched abortion, and although public outcry demanded the "doctor" who performed the procedure be tried for murder, his identity remained unknown.

Peter Wilds died on January 12, 1899 and is buried in Lake Forest Cemetery, Grand Haven, Michigan. His wife passed away in 1948.

REVEREND ERIC P. OLLSON

The Reverend Eric Peter Ollson was the *only* Lutheran minister who agreed to administer the holy sacrament to Frederick Hollman before he was hanged. Ollson appeared at Hollman's jail cell the night before the day of his execution.

Ollson was the leader of the Swedish Lutheran Church in Paxton, Illinois.

The Paxton Record newspaper published an editorial criticizing Lutheran ministers who they claimed had not done enough to minister to the condemned man for the sake of his soul.

Hollman said in his final statement that it was through the acts of Professor Blome and Reverend Wilson that he "was saved" in his final moments, but Ollson's role, while understated, was significant.

Ollson believed he was "not to judge" Hollman, as that authority rested with God almighty. He broke bread and shared wine with Hollman, Blome, and Wilson in the jail cell before midnight on May 13, 1897.

Ollson was born on November 24, 1857 in Undersvik, Helsingland, Sweden. He immigrated to America with his parents, John and Martha Ollson, in 1870. He resided in Pennsylvania and Kansas for a time before moving to Rock

Island, Illinois where he attended Augustana College and Theological Seminary from 1880-87.

He became the pastor of the Swedish Lutheran Church in Paxton in December 1888 and served there until April 1906. Ollson was married to Miss Esther Thorstenberg on May 18, 1893. The couple had three sons and three daughters.

Ollson went on to pastor the Swedish Lutheran Church in Falun, Kansas. He died on March 8, 1928 at the age of 70 and is buried at the Assaria Lutheran Church Cemetery in Aline County, Kansas with his wife and two of their children.

FINAL WITNESSES TO PASS AWAY

The longest surviving witnesses called at the trial of Frederick Hollman were likely James Milton Grant and Faye M. Preston. Grant died in 1968, Preston in 1970.

James Milton Grant had testified at Hollman's trial that he believed he had met him on the road December 2, 1896, the day Wiebke Geddes was murdered.

"I cannot say positively that this is the man," Grant said at trial. He described accurately Hollman's attire and said the man told him he was headed to the Stuhmer farm to see about acquiring a job to shuck feed corn.

Milton died at the age of 90 on September 14, 1968 in Montgomery, Ohio.

Faye Murr Preston, a 13-year-old student, discovered a wash basin beneath the porch of the Ashley schoolhouse the afternoon on the day of Wiebke Geddes' murder.

Hollman reportedly used the basin to wash blood from his face and hands after killing Wiebke Geddes.

Faye Preston went on to become a teacher at that school. She never married. Preston taught primary grades in Gibson City, Melvin and Decatur elementary schools where she had moved by 1945. She died on August 14, 1970 at the age of 87 and is buried in the Gibson City Cemetery.

CARRIE LENZ' STOLEN GOLD WRIST WATCH

One artifact connected to murder of Carrie Lenz remained hidden for nearly three years until it was discovered the end of August 1899. It was the gold wrist watch owned by woman, which was stolen from her when she was killed.

The watch was found in the Stuhmer farmhouse where Frederick Hollman was staying at the time of his arrest on December 6, 1896.

A news dispatch from Paxton, Illinois the final days of August 1899 stated Lenz' gold watch had been discovered "in the tick of Hollman's bed" by Hank Stuhmer. It was inside a straw-stuffed mattress for 34 months. Albert Lenz was summoned and positively identified the watch as having belonged to his death wife.

"This (the finding of the missing watch) is an echo of one of the most horrible crimes in the criminal annals of this country," the Grand Haven Tribune commented in its September 5, 1899 edition. The newspaper noted the discovery of the dead woman's watch and where it was found left little doubt Hollman was Lenz' killer. "He did this murder, it is sure," the Tribune said.

Albert Lenz handed the watch down to his daughter, Florence Lenz (Schmid). Florence gave it to her son, Charles E. Schmid. Charles died in 1998 and the watch remains in the possession of his wife, Constance Schmid, who is in her mid-80s. According to her son, the item is locked away in a safety deposit box at a local bank.

OTHER ARTIFACTS: THE "HANGING" TICKETS AND HOLLMAN'S TRUNK

It has been reported that only three tickets out of 100 printed to the Ford County jailhouse execution of May 14, 1897 survive today and are at the Ford County Museum. They bear the names of T. D. Thompson, E. A Gardner, and A. A. Moffett.

Thomas D. Thompson, 50-years-old at the time, was a postmaster in Melvin. Edmund A. Gardner, age 36 at the time, was at one time a county superintendent of schools for Ford County. August A. Moffet was a juror in the Hollman trial.

The ticket bearing the name of Edmund A. Gardner was discovered at a Pennsylvania flea market in May 1988 and given to the Ford County Historical Society. It was in mint condition, and no one is sure how it ended up there.

There is a photograph of another ticket. The original ticket itself is missing. It was issued to Charles Bogardus, a 56-year old Real Estate and Loan Broker.

According to reports, Frederick Hollman gave his Attorney Columbus Schneider a wooden trunk in appreciation of his services. It was said to be Hollman's "only possession" at the time of his hanging. The trunk, which was stored in Schneider's attic at home for some time, was reportedly given to Sheriff Fred R. Kemp by Mrs. Schneider. It was said to have been in display in the Paxton Courthouse for some time.

PART 11

The Hollman Story Today

Beginning in 2007, descendants of Frederick William Hollman began extensive research of their genealogy. Leading the effort was a woman who was a great-great granddaughter of Frederick Hollman, with assistance from two great-great nephews.

Also helping was the woman's mother, who was the great granddaughter of Frederick Hollman.

Descendants kept running into a roadblock when it came to Augusta Pauline Rohde's first husband, Frederick Hollman. It was unlike her second marriage to Herman Boettcher, which was well documented.

"We always thought that Augusta Pauline Rhode's first husband's name was William," the great-great granddaughter said.

The difficulty for these ancestors in finding information on Frederick William Hollman was due to two factors.

The first was all of aliases the Hollman had used after leaving his wife and children in 1892.

The second was that Augusta (Rhode) Hollman never revealed to her two children, Herman and Minnie, who their father actually was or how he had met his demise.

"My mom told me that the story she grew up knowing," Hollman's great-great granddaughter said. "That Fred William was killed in a railroad accident in the Chicago area. I can see why my ancestor (Augusta Hollman) came up with that story."

Augusta Hollman sought to protect her two children, and the story of their birth father being "killed in a train accident" endured until November 2010 when research for this book connected this author with Hollman's descendants.

After nearly 114 years, they discovered the secret that Frederick Hollman had been hanged for committing murder.

"Who would want to tell anyone you were related to a person like that?" the great-great granddaughter said, in regards to Augusta Hollman's revision of family history.

When other descendants of Frederick Hollman were informed of their relative's true past, they were equally shocked at the discovery.

"You hear of all sorts of stories people find when they do genealogy research. You know, skeletons in the closet. But all of this seriously puts that to shame," the great-great granddaughter said. "I have discussed all of this at length with my mom (Minnie Hollman's daughter.) We don't have your typical skeleton in the closet. We've got a serial killer in our closet."

Knowing that Frederick William Hollman beat and nearly killed her great-great grandmother Augusta made the descendant aware of her own existence.

"I'm so very very glad that my great-great grandmother Augusta was able to get the hell away from Fred," she said. "Or otherwise, I wouldn't even be here."

The descendants were particularly disturbed about the information regarding the Geddes murder where the woman's 6-year-old daughter Elizabeth was found at the scene sitting on a bed. The little girl had witnessed the murder of her mother, and had been choked herself.

"The things that little girl must have went through in her life. To be a witness to the murder of her mother by that evil man," the great-great granddaughter said. "I feel so bad, sad, and ashamed to have to admit that that man was my great-great grandfather."

Frederick Hollman's two children, Minnie and Herman, went to their graves without ever knowing who their birth father was.

"And, let me tell you," the descendant added. "Minnie Hollman was a sweetheart of a lady." Minnie died in 1981.

Another great-great granddaughter of Frederick Hollman, in her mid-60s and living near Detroit, Michigan, was soon informed of the "family secret."

She traveled to Grand Haven in April 2011 to see her descendant's former home town. It was revealed that while the "family secret" may be out, it is still guarded to a lesser degree. "Not everyone (in the family) knows," she said.

This woman joined a meeting of Grand Haven's Dusty Dozens historical group in the Spring of 2011 for a discussion about Frederick Hollman. While attending the gathering, she was asked how she felt about having such a disturbing descendant.

"It is what it is," she said. The woman explained as much as she was shocked and saddened by her great-great grandfather's deeds, it was a fact and a part of history. "Information, the good and the bad, is recorded," she added. "There's nothing we can do to change that."

The woman visited Lake Forest Cemetery at the location of Frederick Hollman's empty grave. It is where Hollman wished to be buried, but was denied. Hollman's first wife Amelia and their two children are buried there.

The descendants' names remain anonymous out of respect for their privacy.

What comes now is a second healing process for all of those who know the truth.

It is a healing process Augusta Pauline Hollman first knew with her decision to spare her children the truth, seeking to bury it for all time.

Kevin Collier

Descendants of persons mentioned in this book were also located during research for this project. Included is a member of the Stroh family, a descendant of a juror at the trial, and ancestors of Bertha Hilgendorf and Carrie Lenz, two of the murdered women.

Gail Hahn Hutchcraft is a descendant of the Stroh family, who owned the farm that was the location of Wiebke Geddes's murder. Her great grandfather, "Chris" (Andrea Christian) Stroh testified at the Hollman trail. Her grandfather, "Fred" (Andreas Ferdinand) Stroh worked nearly at the Claus Stroh farm but was at the murder scene after it occurred. Hutchcraft, her mother and sister lived with Fred and his wife Minnie from 1945 to 1954.

"My grandfather didn't talk much, he was so hard of hearing and meek," Hutchcraft said. "The story wasn't that interesting to me at the time. I guess and I doubt I ever asked questions."

Rosemary Kurtz's great-great grandfather William Wallace Reser was a juror in the Hollman trial. Reser died in 1917. While she never met him, her grandmother's house was next door to Hollman's defense attorney Columbus S. Schneider. Kurtz, a Paxton Carnegie Library Historian, recalled playing in the attic of the Schneider's home.

"Mattie (Mrs. Schneider) let me play in the attic," Kurtz recalled. "She kept her beautiful black dress covered with black jet beads that she wore to one of President Roosevelt's Inaugural balls up there along with the inaugural invitation and other memorabilia. To a little girl, it was like Cinderella all over the place."

Mattie Schneider gave Rosemary Kurtz some of her husband's history books, which are still in her possession. "He (Columbus) was fascinated with Tom Thumb, and had all kinds of pictures of him," Kurtz added. "He kept those in the trunk."

Donald Hilgendorf, whose great grandmother Bertha Hilgendorf was said to have been murdered by Frederick Hollman was unaware of the revelations concerning his great grandfather, August Hilgendrof, who was convicted of the murder and spent the last years of his life in the Wisconsin State prison in Waupun. His grandfather, Oscar Hilgendorf, was one of the two sons who testified at August Hilgendorf's trial. "It is a distinct possibility," Donald said, addressing information that his ancestor was considered to be an innocent man. He explained his parents did not reveal much to him about this family tragedy. "Later in their lives, my parents alluded to something 'bad' happening in Racine, Wisconsin," Hilgendorf said. "But, nothing specific... This whole episode is like a fiction novel."

Bret Schmid is the great grandson of Carrie Lenz, who was murdered by Frederick Hollman on Thanksgiving Day, 1896, in Gilman, Illinois. The story has survived for generations in the family.

"He (Hollman) worked for Albert Lenz at one time," Schmid said, referring to a year before and year of the murder of his great grandmother. "They found my grandmother's watch in the mattress of the bed where he was staying when they arrest him."

Schmid relayed that even though the tragedy has stayed with the family, it didn't cause his great grandfather, Albert Lenz to move on. "We've been here for way over 100 years."

Schmidt recalls his grandmother, Florence Lenz (Schmid), and how she possessed the gold watch Hollman had stolen from the Albert Lenz residence the day Carrie Lenz was murdered.

Florence, the daughter of Carrie Lenz, was no more than six months old when her mother was killed. She died on March 26, 1981 at the age of 84.

"She (Florence) gave the watch to my mother," Schmid said. "Mom still has it in a lock box."

In 2011, the After Dark Paranormal team received permission to investigate the old Ford County jailhouse. They would conduct two investigations, the first of which took place on May 14, the anniversary of Frederick Hollman's hanging.

However, the date was not intentional, but by coincidence. The team had heard tales of a man who was hanged there over 100 years ago, but did not know the day on which he was hanged nor details of his victims.

It would be after this first investigation that the team stumbled across the information and story behind Frederick Hollman during the writing of this book, and explicit details of who the man was, his victims, and his hanging on May 14, 1897 was shared with team members.

This compelled a second investigation on August 13, and the results of the findings might support Hollman's claim that he would come back from the dead to haunt those who had condemned him to hang.

After he was sentenced to death, Hollman spoke in regards to those who he felt were responsible.

"Just wait until I am dead and I will come back every night and visit those men who put me here, those witnesses and jurors," Hollman said. "I will haunt then to their graves. I will rap on their windows at night, and they will see my face at their windows."

One particular piece of evidence the paranormal team captured was a photograph of the outside of the Ford County jailhouse of the second story window, where Hollman's cell had been. "Our evidence included a photo with a face in the window that looked remarkably like Mr. Hollman," said Vickie Craig, a team investigator.

Upon examination, the photo does appear to show the faint image of a man wearing a mustache, resembling Hollman, peering out from the window.

Craig had been at the jailhouse earlier that year on January 28 was present at the May 14 and August 13 investigations.

According to team investigator Terry Garlock, the group even went so far as to suspend a rope and noose from a rafter at the precise location in the room Hollman was hanged.

KII devices, which measure electromagnetic fields believed to indicate a paranormal presence, responded positively.

"A lot of KII action occurred inside his (Hollman's jail) cell, which looked out to the area where the gallows would've been built," Garlock said. "Inside his cell, I did a very creative reading of his poem, 'Legendary,' and at the end the KII's were on full red, which is the highest reading it can give."

"Legendary" was the title of the unfinished poem that Frederick Hollman wrote in the hours before his execution. It read:

> *My name is Frederick Hoellman,*
> *I come from a far off country,*
> *Which follows the river Rhine,*
> *To America I journeyed*
> *In honest to toll,*
> *And now they gonna hang me,*
> *And raise a great turmoil.*
> *On 14 day of May,*
> *When flowers are in bloom,*
> *Between sunrise and sunset,*
> *I must meet my fatal doom.*
> *They said I did a murder,*
> *but that I will deny....*

The poem left off at those words, never completed. It has been published in a few select writings concerning Hollman's execution as being the only capital punishment case in Ford County, Illinois history. Some versions of the poem use the phrase "final doom."

"We started asking what he did with the pocket watch (he reportedly stole from victim Carrie Lenz) and the straight razor (he reportedly stole owned by victim Wiebke Geddes' husband Fred). Both items that were taken from the murder scenes but never turned up," Garlock explained. "The KII's dropped down to green lights, until I snapped off a string of sentences in German I learned as a child."

"When Terry started ranting in German, the atmosphere really changed within the cell that we were sitting," Craig said. "The KIIs went off and several of us that are sensitive felt it."

"It (speaking in German) caused all of the KII meters to jump to red lights and other team members present in the jail cell and nearby to jump."

Craig pointed to EVPs (electronic voice phenomenon) and words from an Ovilus as supporting evidence of paranormal responses.

EVPs are voices or sounds captured on a digital recorder, which can be played back. An Ovilus is a hand-held instrument that is designed to interpret energies or magnetic fields that are assimilated into words, which the devise can pronounce as audio the operator can hear or the word displayed on a display screen for the operator to see.

Vickie Craig explained that on the May 14, 2011 investigation at the Ford County jailhouse, the team went in knowing nothing about Frederick Hollman or his crimes. The most the team knew was a man had been hanged there, but the evidence collected that night would later correlate with historic details.

The most interesting was the information we got on the Ovulis," Craig explained. "We got names, mainly women's names. The name that came a lot was Amelia and Carrie. The name Elizabeth came around as well, and Anna a few times. Also, words such as 'rope,' 'hurt,' 'death' came up a lot, and at the time, none of this made any sense to us."

Soon after this, After Dark Paranormal members discovered that this book about Frederick Hollman being written, and the "words" strangely correlated with the historic record.

"Amelia" was the name of Frederick Hollman's first wife, the woman he wished to be buried next to in Grand Haven, Michigan, a request that was not honored after his execution.

"Carrie" was the name of the fourth murder victim attributed to Hollman, Carrie Lenz.

"Elizabeth" was the name of Elizabeth Mary Schertz, the only woman whom Hollman tried to strange and escaped to tell the tale.

"Anna" was the name of Anna Catherine Mohr, the third murder victim attributed to Hollman.

The words "rope," "hurt," and "death" need no explanation.

At the August 13 investigation, armed with historic information from this book, they were able to ask about details of Hollman's life, crimes, and victims.

"We asked about the watch that was missing," Craig said, which was reportedly stolen by Hollman from the home of Albert Lenz, owned by victim Carrie. "The Ovulis simply responded, 'lost.'"

Also at the August 13 investigation was psychic and medium Rick Hayes.

"Rick talked alot about his (Hollman's) mother and asked how she would feel with all this knowledge of his life," Craig said, describing the attempt to provoke a spirit of the killer. "This seemed to not set well with Hollman. During this time, as well as the time we were doing a session where he was actually hung, we got knocks and sounds during the EVP time there."

When it comes to paranormal research, perhaps Hollman did make good on his threat to "rap" on things. Names were spoken, apparently by an entity, that connects to the killer's history.

One might be wary of looking up at a second story window of the abandoned, historic Ford County jailhouse after dark. Remember, as Hollman said, "they will see my face at their windows."

114 years after that warning, the team of paranormal investigators agree, they saw just that.

Kevin Scott Collier, 55, is the author and/or illustrator of over 100 books for children and teens. He began his career as an author in 2004 with his first published book, the critically acclaimed *barthpenn@ heaven.org*. He recently wrote and illustrated a book series for the "Tanked" TV programs, which airs on the Animal Planet Network. Collier has also a graphic designer and columnist for the Grand Haven Tribune newspaper for over 30 years and is a member of the Dusty Dozens historical group of Ottawa County, Michigan.

In the past few years, Collier released a series of books titled "Strange Grand Haven" based on paranormal stories and folklore originating in and surrounding his hometown. The theme has also become a weekly column in the daily newspaper Collier works for. Today, he lives with his wife and son near the shore of Lake Michigan in Grand Haven, Michigan.

A history buff of the strange and unusual, Collier was struck by news in Grand Haven Tribune newspaper microfilm files from 1897 of a former resident of his hometown who moved on to become one of our nation's first serial killers. He attempted to uncover more about the man, Frederick Hollman, but found virtually no record of the man, thus decided to write a book on American's overlook killer. The research involved digging through countless historical newspapers, records, transcripts and uncovered many descendants of victims in the story. The result is *Final Doom: The Frederick Hollman Story*, which took over two years to compile and write.

CPSIA information can be obtained at www.ICGtesting.com
Printed in the USA
BVOW071215041112

304632BV00001B/42/P